Emerging Trends in Real Estate® Europe

20 11

Contents

Editorial Leadership Team

Emerging Trends in Real Estate® Europe 2011 Chairs
Patrick L. Phillips, Urban Land Institute
Kees Hage, PwC (Luxembourg)

Principal Authors and Advisers
Lucy Scott, Urban Land Institute Consultant
John Forbes, PwC (U.K.)
Dirk Brounen, PwC Consultant (the Netherlands)
Lydia Westrup, Urban Land Institute Consultant

Principal Researchers and Advisers
Stephen Blank, Urban Land Institute
Charles J. DiRocco, Jr., PwC (U.S.)
Dean Schwanke, Urban Land Institute

ULI Adviser
Alex Notay, Urban Land Institute

Recommended bibliographic listing:
Urban Land Institute and PwC. Emerging Trends in Real Estate® Europe 2011. Washington, D.C.: Urban Land Institute, 2011

ULI Catalog Number: E43
ISBN: 978-0-87420-155-0

Cover photos, clockwise from top left: Mumuth, Graz, Austria (Rob Hoekstra); Citilab, Barcelona, Spain (Isidor Fernández); Mumuth, Graz, Austria (Iwan Bahn); Palazzo Tornabuoni, Florence, Italy (Roberto Quagli).

PwC Advisers and Contributing Researchers

Austria: Markus Brugger, Rudolf Schmid, Monika Urbanitzky

Belgium: Grégory Jurion, Sandra Pascual Vallés, Maarten Tas, Nancy Van de Voorde

Cyprus: Vassilis Vizas

Czech Republic: Richard Jones, Glen Lonie

Denmark: Janni Guldager, Jakob Hermann, Jesper Wiinholt

Finland: Niko Kivelä

France: Benoît Audibert, Sandrine Berbel, Fabrice Bricker, Jean-Baptiste Deschryver, Daniel Fesson, Antoine Grenier, Bettina Laville, Bruno Lunghi, Geoffroy Schmitt, Béatrice Theiller

Germany: Sven Behrends, Jochen Bruecken, Susanne Eickermann-Riepe, Dirk Hennig, Johannes Schneider, Thomas von Cölln

Greece: Ioannis Petrou, Vassilis Vizas

Ireland: Enda Faughnan

Italy: Christine Barrozo Savignon, Gloria Bertin, Margherita Biancheri, Elisabetta Caldirola, Giovanni Ferraioli, Salvatore Grasso, Alberto Londi, Michelangelo Pepe, Lorenzo Pini Prato, Alessandro Raone, M. Savicevic, Lia Turri, Elena Valente, Claudia Varano

Luxembourg: Julien Sporgitas, Vassilis Vizas

Norway: Vibeke Hove Monsen Krogh

Poland: Kinga Barchoń, Jakub Jonkisz, Grażyna Wiejak-Roy

Portugal: Jorge Figueiredo, Elsa Silva Martins

Romania: Brian Arnold

Russia: Antonin Busta, Richard James Gregson, Marina Kharitidi

Spain: Iñigo Aldaz Pérez, Carlos Alvarez Morales, Julian Bravo Cuervo, David Calzada Criado, Paulino de Evan, Javier Gómez Olmedo, Guillermo Massó, Carlos Molero, Miguel Rodríguez de Cepeda, Antonio Sánchez Recio, Gonzalo Sanjurjo Pose

Sweden: Mats Andersson, Johan Björk, Helena Ehrenborg, Göran Engvall, Robert Fonovich, Rikard Jacobsson, Glen Lonie, Ulf Pettersson, Maria Sahlén, Robert Treutiger, Elin Waher

Switzerland: Kurt Ritz, Sven Schaltegger

The Netherlands: Brian Adams, Petra Bangma, Jelle Bas Boon, Michael Bax, Meta Beemer, Caroline Beijdorff, John Brouwer, Maurits Cammeraat, Hans Copier, Serge de Lange, Jeroen Elink Schuurman, Sander Frissen, Joop Kluft, Frank Kraus, Bart Kruijssen, Rogier Mattousch, Christianne Noordermeer Van Loo, Willeke Ong, Bert Oosterloo, Jens Osinga, Gerard Ottenhoff, Wanda Otto, Adamo Ritmeester, Robert Tieskens, Teun van der Made, Sven van Loon

United Kingdom: Sandra Dowling, Holly Folan, Chris Jackson, Chris Mutch, Rosalind Rowe, Gerry Young

ULI Editorial and Production Staff
James Mulligan, Managing Editor/Manuscript Editor
Betsy VanBuskirk, Creative Director
Anne Morgan, Graphic Designer
Craig Chapman, Director of Publishing Operations

Executive Summary

Regulation, Austerity Europe, the sovereign debt crisis, and a lending market that seems weaker than ever are the challenges facing Europe's real estate industry in 2011.

Last year, a series of curveballs were thrown at the industry. First came Greece and its debt woes; then Basel III came for the banks; then Ireland proved that the sovereign debt crisis was far from over; and all the while, the efforts of Europe's politicians to steam clean the financial system with regulation made the industry wonder what else was around the corner.

What *Emerging Trends Europe* interviewees do know for sure is that while the recovery may be underway, it has just become significantly more complicated.

To what extent will Basel III alter the face of real estate finance? Which stressed European economy will be next to seek financial aid? How will spending cuts affect the consumer, businesses, and the fundamental demand for property? These are the questions facing the industry today.

Nobody really knows whether the pressures being felt now could actually be long-term structural shifts that will change the shape of the industry for years to come. But the smartest industry players are adapting in the event that they are.

Persistent sickness in the debt market—which could be considered a generous assessment given that one interviewee described it as "utterly dead"—is a familiar theme for 2011.

That is not surprising given the scale of the problem. What has changed is that while last year's interviewees were angst ridden that the large amount of debt maturing across Europe over the next five years would prevent banks from undertaking new lending, the new questions for 2011 are how much impact Basel III will have on the appetite of banks to lend to property and, when they do, how expensive it will be.

This sense of foreboding has replaced the optimism felt by interviewees in the first half of 2010 that the debt markets were finally becoming friendlier.

There are slim flickers of hope that new sources of debt will come forth—from insurance companies and mezzanine lenders; some even foretell the arrival of Chinese banks. But the consensus view is that even if new players do emerge, they will take a long while to do so and will only partially relieve congestion.

Improvements in the availability of real estate equity are anticipated this year, and this is expected to come from an increasing number of investors from Asia Pacific, institutions, and private equity funds.

But as is the case with so many positive trends today, they do not constitute unqualified good news. Equity, which is now choosier and risk averse, will be funnelled towards a smaller slice of the industry, ensuring that the capital-raising environment is set to be tough for a while yet.

Interviewees anticipate that it is the well-established firms with defensive strategies that will benefit, while for niche or new players, life will remain difficult in 2011. This is just one way the market will continue to divide between the haves and the have-nots over the coming months.

The bifurcation being seen in the industry even extends to employment prospects. The industry will continue to downsize in 2011, interviewees say, and as firms prioritize resources, there will be those in the industry who find their skills in demand and those who find they are totally unequipped for the new climate.

With capital so risk averse, winning cities like London and Paris will continue to absorb investment as the only places where tenant demand will be robust. Meanwhile, cities such as Dublin will be deserted by investors.

But within those winning cities and across countries, capital will home in on the best buildings. The result is that values for secondary properties will remain at distressed levels and decline further in the months ahead. Given that almost one-third of Europe's €960 billion outstanding commercial real estate debt is secured against poor-quality property at high loan-to-value ratios, interviewees believe the real headaches for the banks are about to begin.

While all property sectors show improved investment prospects in the quantitative part of the survey, in the interviews, central city offices, street retail, and shopping centres were most frequently cited as offering "modestly good" prospects.

Despite fears over the impact of Austerity Europe on the consumer, retail takes the lead in the sector rankings, followed by offices; for-rent apartments—last year's top segment—dropped into third place. There is a noticeable gap between these gold medallists and the also-ran sectors—hotels, mixed use, industrial/distribution, and for-sale residential.

Developing core assets sparks interest. All property sectors show enhanced development potential, with the top eight identified as holding "fair" prospects. Central offices take the lead, followed by rental apartments and for-sale apartments. But with bank finance only available for assets that are earning cash flow, development of core assets is a strategy that is difficult to pursue.

Innovation will not be achieved by staying safe. Some interviewees say designing strategies on the basis of selecting individual cities is pointless; they believe that all markets present opportunities at the right price. Seeking out assets where capital is scare but where there is potential demand in the future—such as residential land or sheltered housing and nursing homes—is among a handful of ways interviewees are trying to pursue more creative thinking.

Preface

A joint undertaking of the Urban Land Institute (ULI) and PwC, *Emerging Trends in Real Estate® Europe* is a trends and forecast publication now in its eighth edition. The report provides an outlook on European real estate investment and development trends, real estate finance and capital markets, property sectors, metropolitan areas, and other real estate issues.

Emerging Trends in Real Estate® Europe 2011 represents a consensus outlook for the future and reflects the views of more than 600 individuals who completed surveys and/or were interviewed as part of the research process for this report. Interviewees and survey participants represent a wide range of industry experts—investors, developers, property companies, lenders, brokers, and consultants. ULI and PwC researchers personally interviewed 312 individuals, and survey responses were received from 303 individuals whose company affiliations are broken down as follows:

Real estate service firm	26.6%
Private property company or developer	21.9%
Other	19.8%
Institutional/equity investor or investment manager	18.9%
Bank, lender, or securitized lender	6.0%
Publicly listed property company or REIT	6.0%
Homebuilder or residential land developer	0.9%

A list of the interview participants in this year's study appears at the end of this report. To all who helped, the Urban Land Institute and PwC extend sincere thanks for sharing valuable time and expertise. Without the involvement of these many individuals, this report would not have been possible.

Adapt or Die

"The key thing to remember is to look forward and not back."

This year will not be the turnaround year the European real estate industry hoped for, but it will be a year that could change the shape of the industry for a while to come.

The optimism that had been felt by interviewees in 2010 of a U-shaped, V-shaped, or "Nike swoosh–shaped" recovery has waned. "In January 2010, the sunny uplands did not seem too far away, but they do now," said one interviewee. "Optimism dissipated as every month came and went. It was battered by events."

What this year's survey reveals is that hope has been replaced with acceptance that how things are now could be how they are for a long while to come, and the choice is stark: adapt to this new world or die.

Today, the industry is undergoing far-reaching structural changes created by persistent weaknesses in European economies and in the debt markets. In addition, the threat of further shocks from stressed countries such as Italy, Portugal, and Spain loom large in the interviewees' assessments of the year ahead. As they question how all of this will affect the fundamental demand for real estate, strategies are largely becoming defensive. "Whatever my views on the outlook of the market, they are not defined by conviction," one interviewee said. "You could put me on either side of the argument on whether values are going up or down. The market may suffer reversals."

Caught in a climate of uncertainty, confusion, fear, and mistrust, Europe's real estate industry is in the process of redefining itself. The industry must respond to these changes to survive, urge *Emerging Trends Europe* interviewees. "This is the most confusing business environment that I have ever been through in my entire career," said one veteran fund manager. "No one has any answers. But you have

got to adapt. The key thing to remember is to look forward and not back. If you are not doing that, then you are missing the best opportunities in a generation to invest in property in some form—either debt or equity."

Listless economic growth across Austerity Europe will "force changes in investment and development models," while wounded and anxious institutional investors make "leveraged investors and fund managers reinvent themselves." For the debt markets to function properly once again, it will be necessary to "reinvent them."

The sharpest wakeup call in 2011 will be felt in the secondary market, where many believe the real hangover has not yet set in. "I think we should have a permanent change

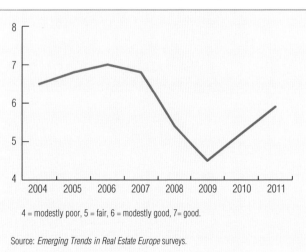

EXHIBIT 1-1
Real Estate Firm Profitability Prospects

4 = modestly poor, 5 = fair, 6 = modestly good, 7= good.

Source: *Emerging Trends in Real Estate Europe* surveys.

EXHIBIT 1-2
Survey Responses by Geographic Scope of Firm

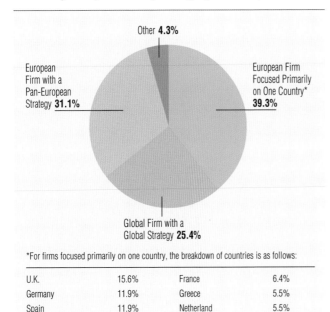

Other **4.3%**

European Firm with a Pan-European Strategy **31.1%**

European Firm Focused Primarily on One Country* **39.3%**

Global Firm with a Global Strategy **25.4%**

*For firms focused primarily on one country, the breakdown of countries is as follows:

U.K.	15.6%	France	6.4%
Germany	11.9%	Greece	5.5%
Spain	11.9%	Netherland	5.5%
Russia	8.3%	Italy	4.6%
Turkey	8.3%	Other Countries	15.6%
Belgium	6.4%		

Source: *Emerging Trends in Real Estate Europe 2011* survey.

EXHIBIT 1-3
Survey Responses by Country

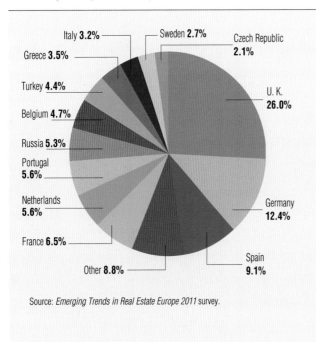

Italy **3.2%**

Sweden **2.7%**

Czech Republic **2.1%**

Greece **3.5%**

Turkey **4.4%**

U. K. **26.0%**

Belgium **4.7%**

Russia **5.3%**

Portugal **5.6%**

Netherlands **5.6%**

Germany **12.4%**

France **6.5%**

Other **8.8%**

Spain **9.1%**

Source: *Emerging Trends in Real Estate Europe 2011* survey.

of mindset. Property is about location and the very basic fundamentals of real estate. A lot of people have been burned by chasing high yields and by being prepared to buy poor-quality assets. It doesn't matter how well you can securitize it and how well you syndicate it, at the end of the day it will still be a pretty ordinary piece of rubbish in the middle of nowhere."

It is, in so many respects, a new world. Survival is a case of do or die, say interviewees. Confusion is no longer an excuse for inertia, and across the industry there are instances of evolution as bored and frustrated developers turn into investors, long-term unemployed deal makers seek out asset management roles they might once have considered too grubby to touch, and fund managers—unable to get the debt to fuel high-risk return strategies—get comfortable with a lower-return environment. And it may be that these very adjustments and adaptations will lead to better performance in 2011. In fact, survey respondents, in spite of the many reservations expressed above, see improved prospects for profitability in 2011 (see exhibit 1-1).

The Haves and the Have-Nots

Interviewees predict that one of the biggest themes for 2011 will be the continued downsizing of the industry.

As firms downsize and prioritize resources, requiring them to focus on certain strategies and skills sets over others, respondents are busy working out how to ensure that they fit into this smaller world.

Job losses in the industry will persist as firms continue a clearing out of the less essential roles in 2011. "We are applying resources where we know activity is happening. There is such a massive concentration of activity in certain markets."

Interviewees believe that many out-of-work real estate professionals will find themselves unequipped for the new climate. "There were too many of us knocking around before. Over the long term, our industry will operate in a much smaller space. The deck is going to be reshuffled." "There is a distinct lack of experience in the market, which is worrying."

Time and time again, interviewees—from bankers to developers, fund managers, and advisers—echoed this sentiment. There was also concern that when it came to moving the industry forward, the innovative people needed in this new landscape were few and far between.

"There is a whole generation of our profession that has never learned how to manage assets. The spreadsheet said it would work, and so they did it. We have plenty of bright sparks, but we need a bit more of that thing called vision. It is a reaction to go defensive, but where are the people who can differentiate themselves?"

This is not just a problem at the top; finding people with the skills to fill the jobs that exist is a challenge right down the food chain. "You can't equate the glut of people out there on the street looking for work with easy pickings.

The right people are harder to find than ever." "Investing in human capital may be necessary. Different skills are needed than were needed four or five years ago." "We have lost a great amount of human capital. There is a lack of experienced people who understand how to manage risk. We need leaders with strategies, not acquisition teams with too much money."

Austerity Europe

Europe's recovery is underway, but interviewees admit it is "hard to feel confident" about the economic picture in 2011.

The more upbeat respondents could only assess the outlook for European economic growth as "flat" over the coming months, with lazy consumer demand and growth, rising taxes, and unemployment all forecast by interviewees.

"We're in a period of two years, maybe longer, where every six months sentiment will swing. There will be times when things get better and when things get worse. After a cataclysm like we have been through, things won't be directional. Recovery will bounce around within a zone."

The European Central Bank will keep interest rates at a record low well into the year, say interviewees, after the bank rounded out 2010 by keeping interest rates at 1 percent. But they will "have to go up sooner or later," predict interviewees. Similarly, inflation is expected to remain subdued throughout 2011, but to rise over the medium term—though with a consumer price index inflation rate of 3.7 percent in the U.K. in December 2010, there could be pressure in the coming months to raise interest rates.

But many respondents described their outlook as "pessimistic," finding it hard to trust positive economic indicators as and when they emerged. "Even when there is good news, there is caution. We could have a double dip [recession] in the U.K.; you can't deny that it is possible. Germany and France could disappoint, and that's why people are reluctant to make decisions." "You can look at the numbers and convince yourself that the world is about to end. The macro economy is bad."

Some even mentioned concerns over a possible breakup of the European Union, especially if Spain and Italy are forced to ask for aid. "How much will core Europe have to bail out weaker countries? I think there's a big risk that we could see the European Union disintegrate."

Anxieties are twofold. First is the fear about how heavily the austerity measures across the region will fall on the consumer, on growth, and on employment. "With rising taxes and shrinking employment, where will growth come from?"

Crucially, no one yet knows how attempts to rebalance economies will fundamentally affect the desire of businesses to expand. "People only increase their desire to occupy property when GDP is increasing, and there are not many places where that is happening." "Under 2 percent growth, all you are doing is filling capacity. If you believe

EXHIBIT 1-4
European Economic Growth

	Percentage Real GDP Growth				
	2012*	2011*	2010*	2009	2008
Russia	5.7	6.0	6.0	5.5	7.0
Turkey	5.3	5.5	5.0	3.0	3.5
Poland	5.0	4.9	4.8	3.8	5.2
Czech Republic	4.5	4.5	4.2	3.4	4.0
Ireland	4.1	4.0	2.5	-0.6	-1.8
Luxembourg	3.9	4.0	3.4	1.8	2.3
Greece	3.5	3.0	2.6	2.0	3.2
Hungary	3.5	3.7	3.0	2.3	1.9
U.K.	3.2	3.3	2.2	-0.1	1.0
Sweden	3.2	3.2	2.8	1.4	1.2
Spain	3.1	2.6	1.8	-0.2	1.4
France	2.8	2.8	1.6	0.2	0.8
Belgium	2.6	2.6	1.9	0.2	1.4
Austria	2.6	2.6	2.1	0.8	2.0
Finland	2.5	2.5	2.2	1.6	2.5
Netherlands	2.2	2.2	1.6	1.0	2.3
Portugal	1.8	1.7	1.0	0.1	0.6
Switzerland	1.8	1.8	1.8	0.7	1.7
Germany	1.5	1.2	1.0	0.0	1.9
Denmark	1.0	0.5	0.4	1.1	1.6
Italy	1.0	0.8	0.3	-0.2	-0.1

Sources: International Monetary Fund; Moody's (www.economy.com).
*Projections.

we will have positive but pedestrian economic growth over the next few years, then that has to have implications on your outlook for occupier markets."

The second anxiety is sovereign weakness weighing on the market as the difference in yield between Europe's benchmark German bunds and ten-year bonds for economies such as Portugal hover around record highs.

Ireland may not be the last economy to require financial aid. In 2011, Europe could lurch from "one bailout to another," said interviewees. "I think one has to be cautious—I wouldn't even say cautiously optimistic. I am not sure we know what effect the disruption in the Eurozone will have on the wider recovery."

While there were few who foresee a double-dip recession, most respondents expect performance in Europe's economies to be "two speed," causing an ever-widening divide between the haves and the have-nots.

These divisions will be seen not only between countries, but also between capital cities and regional markets within the same country. "I am bullish on Europe, but my Europe is core Europe. I don't think about Poland. I think about northern Europe—Scandinavia, Holland, France, and Germany. We have real concerns about investing in peripheral countries. We wonder if those countries will still be in the Eurozone in the future."

The result of these concerns leads some to question Europe's ability to attract capital in a world where Asia is booming and the United States is offering better access to distressed opportunities. "The problem for Europe is we are in a distant third, bronze-medal position. If you are a big pension fund, then you are probably allocating half of your money to Asia, 30 percent to America, and the rest to Europe, and most of that will go to Germany." One fund manager added, "I don't think Europe is flavour of the month for investors. So we are fighting the argument of 'Why should I give money to you when Asia is growing?'"

Be Big or Be Irrelevant

Given the state of Europe's economic outlook, executing strategies was cited as one of the biggest challenges faced by interviewees for 2011. One anticipates "skewed economic results. Nothing is going to be clear. I think you will find value is shifting places. You can't stick with one theme or location in the next few years."

But it is not just that. In all corners of the European real estate industry, businesses are coming up against difficulties in employing strategies that take advantage of the market in the way they want. This is because equity and debt being invested in real estate are homing in on specific, defensive opportunities.

This problem is manifesting itself in several ways. For fund managers, attracting equity to establish new vehicles is the problem—not because there isn't enough money around, but because institutions are being more cautious and focussed. "The capital-raising environment is very slow. It is much more targeted to single-country, single sector–themed funds rather than panregional ones because value is not consistently reliable across regions."

New outfits set up to take advantage of the downturn, as well as niche players, are battling to establish their relevance in a marketplace where equity and debt are seeking a home in big firms or those with a star reputation, and preferably both. "People are trying to reinvent themselves but fundraising is so difficult."

Opportunistic players are having a hard time finding deals at all, let alone at worthwhile returns. "Everyone is chewing their fingernails." Unable to obtain the 20 percent returns they have been accustomed to, many in this section of the market are redefining their return profiles. "What is a good real rate of return for my opportunity fund? Is it 10 percent or is it 15 percent? I think we must educate the investment community about what is a realistic rate of return in light of no debt." "Fifteen is the new 20 percent." But players also complain that the opportunity business "has been irreparably damaged by a few funds which have behaved appallingly," and, therefore, raising capital for new funds is "extremely tough."

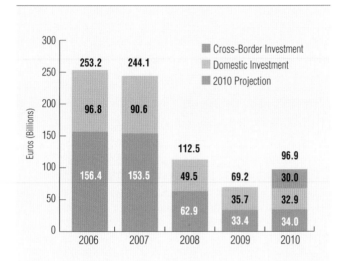

EXHIBIT 1-5
European Direct Real Estate Investment

Source: Jones Lang LaSalle.

Note: Cross-border investment activity is defined as any direct transaction that involves a foreign buyer or seller.

Except for big developers with a major pre-lease and a partner, lack of interest from banks promises to keep most developers underemployed for 2011. "More equity is required. You can dream about 60 percent leverage, but you better be prepared to go with 50 percent. For speculative stuff, most development is just not possible. In London, Paris, Frankfurt, and Munich, you could get financing for the right locations, however." Prompted by lack of opportunities, some are taking the opportunity to evolve into investment management.

Listed property companies, while identified by interviewees as one of the stronger market players today given the appetite for core investment and their ability to raise capital, are challenged by a shareholder base whose ambitions are increasingly global.

Interviewees anticipate that investors who buy shares will not bother differentiating between individual companies in Europe, preferring to buy the index instead because Europe's listed property sector is just a small part of the overall global property sector. "The scary thing is that Europe's listed property sector is only 15 percent of EPRA's [European Public Real Estate Association] global index. Increasingly, mandates are going global. Investors are saying, 'Why bother going into stock selection? We will just invest in the index instead.' So be big or be irrelevant in the European listed space."

Diamonds in the Rough

For safety, many respondents are defensively sticking to core strategies—and this lack of confidence for anything else is anticipated to remain a major theme for 2011. As one fund manager noted, "The minute you leave the core segment, what are the future scenarios you can assume in putting together an investment case? What bank terms will you get in 2012, 2013? Who knows?"

Therefore, the focus for 2011 for many is on just a few "winning" cities and countries where occupational demand will be firmer. "Outside of the U.K., France, and Germany, the main markets will be Sweden, Poland, Italy, and Spain, and nothing else is worth having a conversation about," said one interviewee. "It will be a long time before institutions and family offices venture beyond prime cities. There is a lot of real estate that will never be occupied again. I am very worried about secondary high street, poorly managed industrial, or 1960s- or 1970s-built provincial offices."

But even in the core space, there are risks. Some perceive that the competition for core is so frenzied that pricing has reached unfathomable levels. This is especially true in London and Paris, but respondents claim bidding wars for assets in markets such as the Czech Republic are being run by advisers "like it was 2006."

"This quickly after the crash we are pricing things at perfection again. Everyone knows this is a manufactured-interest-rate environment, and people are pricing deals off of it. What's to say we won't have 6 percent interest rates in a few years?

Why buy something at a 6 percent yield when interest rates could be 6 percent? You can't inflate yourself out of that."

But there are those who are trying to navigate away from the crowded market to pursue more creative strategies. Interviewees' top tip for finding value in today's market is to seek out situations where capital is scarce but where there is also potential for demand for product in due course. Here are some of the most interesting strategies interviewees are pursuing that are based on that idea:

Buy land: "We are putting money into buying strategic residential land sites. At the moment, U.K. house builders are not putting much money into land, but there will be continued demand for housing."

Help the aged: For security of long-term income, look to provide assets that cater to different phases in life, such as sheltered housing, nursing homes and, student accommodation.

Buy good-quality secondary: Buy better-quality secondary property when it is artificially discounted to prime. "When the markets recover, you will see a recovery in good-quality secondary. The market reclassifies what is prime and blurs secondary, so if you can, buy that stock cleverly with the right sort of yield discount."

Work with Spanish banks: "There are a lot of syndications in Spain with overseas banks, and these syndicates have heavy restructuring to do. Some banks can't do that, so they want out. Slowly there are things that will get undone and these banks will exit these countries. We may get involved alongside Spanish banks in restructuring."

Complete unfinished projects: "If we undertake development in Paris or London, then we could probably capture a rental increase in prime space. There is very little finance around for that, but slowly there will be some seller finance from banks that are trying to get rid of developments. We can come in and help complete projects that were not finished when the crisis hit."

Resilient Economies

Resilient markets economically are considered to be the U.K., France, and the Nordic countries, with export-led Germany being cited time and again by respondents as the leader of the pack. Its fast-paced recovery through 2010 and a declining unemployment rate, which currently sits at 6.7 percent, provided reasons for optimism.

"Germany is doing remarkably well. Germany builds things people want." "Germany is performing better than people thought they would a few years ago. It will continue to be strong. It has an extremely stable outlook." Interviewees assess Germany's current strength as being driven by demand from emerging markets, especially China. While some question whether that can be sustained over the long term, "it is still a place to invest in."

EXHIBIT 1-6
Strategic Investment Allocation Preferences for 2011

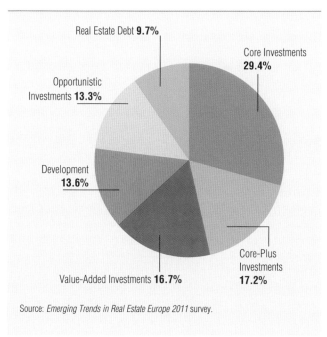

Source: *Emerging Trends in Real Estate Europe 2011* survey.

But interviewees point out that while Germany's economic recovery has been relatively robust, its real estate market has not experienced the same level of interest as that of the U.K. The country's good economic prospects make its retail sector particularly attractive for investors in Europe, the survey reveals (see chapter 4).

"While Germany is doing very well from a general economic standpoint, real estate market activity in Germany is still very muted." "We should take advantage of the situation in Germany as it has a strong economy. Tenants in London have taken advantage of the situation and have used vacancies as leverage for securing more space with lower rents. But this hasn't happened in Germany yet."

In the U.K., interviewees say that while the country has benefitted from not being part of the euro, there is now polarization between London and the rest of the country. "The effect of the [spending] cuts will come through over the next 18 months. It is easy to have a rosy view of U.K. walking around near your London office where restaurants are full, but I suspect in a place like Middlesbrough you'd see a different view."

Interviewees believe the U.K. government, with the luxury of having no election around the corner, will be able to push through "more savage cuts" that will strangle consumption and employment. While there is hope in some surveys that the private sector will be able to make up for job losses in the public sector, some believe that "the political imperative is not to encourage businessmen and bankers to get risky." "The problem is that cuts are being made, but ideas for stimulating growth are missing."

Concerns over how public sector job cuts will affect regional cities such as Newcastle loom large as Prime Minister David Cameron seeks to close the budget deficit. "The discrepancy between London and the regions will get even bigger. The U.K. will become more like France and become more centralised."

Many fear the U.K. recession has not really arrived yet. Some fear that even though interest rates may stay low in 2011, an increase "cannot be far away," given the news that inflation had jumped to 3.7 percent in December. "The downturn has hit a lot of bankers, but the man on the street hasn't been adversely affected yet. As jobs cut back, people won't be able to spend. People with mortgages have been better off in the last couple of years than in 2007. They have had more disposable income than a few years ago." "I don't see how office rental growth happens at all in the U.K. for the next few years outside of London."

Therefore, interviewees are wary of anything outside of London and the South East. "London will keep going. Investment demand and demand for good-quality space will continue there. But the regional markets will remain pretty flat. Some specific places exposed to government tenants will have an even more tricky time. We will have a two-speed U.K. for a long time."

Interviewees characterize France as "stable but not booming," displaying "slow growth, but growth nonetheless." Surveys and analysts expect GDP growth to pick up slowly through 2011, led by business investment and exports, as unemployment declines slightly. Surveys reveal an investment focus on Paris, where the occupier market is expected to remain healthy. But some interviewees point out that France's regional cities are performing better than those in the U.K.: "In Lyon, Marseille, Bordeaux, and Toulouse there are reasonable levels of demand from the occupational market."

Interviewees also said the Nordics are regarded as stable and a "solid environment for investment," while consumer spending in Turkey is expected to remain robust. Meanwhile, Poland garnered the most effusive responses. "We are extremely bullish on Poland. We think about Poland as a separate market in central-eastern Europe because the economic fundamentals are better, it has a highly skilled workforce, and less and less corruption." "I don't see Poland's great run ending."

Stressed Economies

Sitting in the really unpopular camp are Italy, Ireland, Portugal, and Greece with their high levels of either public or private debt, and in some cases both. Respondents predict some potential "crisis scenarios" in 2011 from these stressed economies—a sentiment that chimes with analyst warnings that the European Union could be forced to rescue more member states over the coming months.

Big concerns in the interviews centre on Italy, where intense government intervention has created an "artificial sense of security," and Spain, where respondents fear its efforts to avoid rescue through raising taxes, slashing wages, and privatizing state industries may not pay off.

"The one to watch is Italy. It worries me. It has the biggest amount of debt and is horribly managed. You can argue that Greece is a disaster, but it doesn't matter economically. Italy does; it is big." If Italy falls, it could create another Lehman Brothers–style shock, some say. "Italy should introduce an austerity programme and, more importantly, implement it."

But many interviewees loyally believe Spain will eventually find its footing and argue that, like London, the streets of Madrid and Barcelona belie the economic indicators and press reports. "The biggest mistake that people made about Spain in 1996 was that people were too conservative about its potential. The fundamental demographics are positive. Construction was the excess of growth, but some components of the construction industry remain relevant for Spain. That which was linked to building was a negative, but infrastructure is still needed. That will have a positive effect in Spain."

EXHIBIT 1-7

European Cross-Border Real Estate Investment by Country of Origin

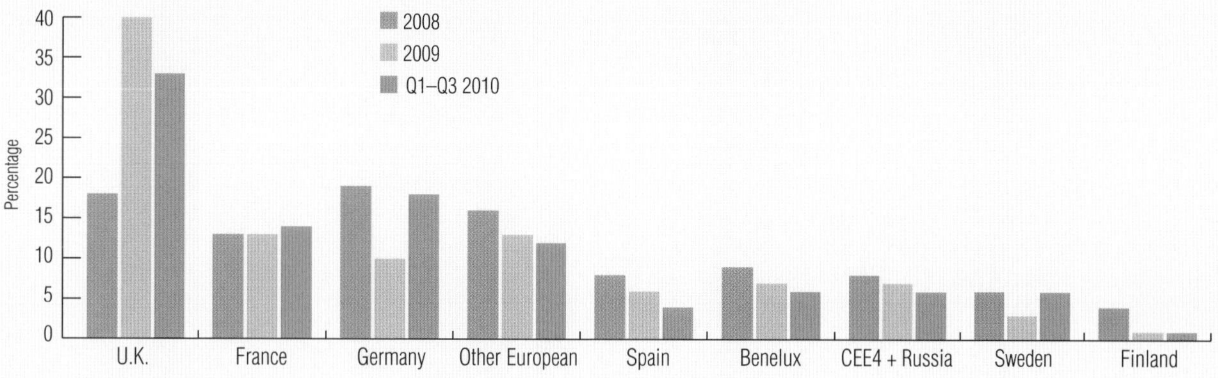

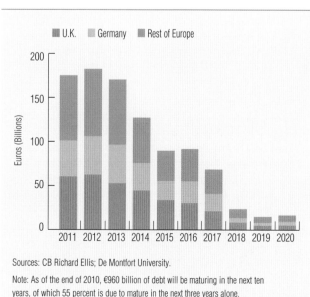

Legend:
- 2008
- 2009
- Q1–Q3 2010

Categories (Percentage): U.K., France, Germany, Other European, Spain, Benelux, CEE4 + Russia, Sweden, Finland

Source: Jones Lang LaSalle.

Note: CEE4 (Central and Eastern Europe 4) is the Czech Republic, Hungary, Poland, and Slovakia.

The Debt Drought Continues

The reduction in the lending capacity of banks in real estate is a feature of the European real estate industry for the foreseeable future and one that continues to put a limit on the number of people who can play in the market, interviewees warn.

"The debt markets in Europe are utterly dead," said one. "The Pfandbrief banks have taken a meaningful step backwards. There are more French banks lending than German banks. The Irish, U.K., Italian, and Spanish banks are lending zero. One or two Scandinavian banks will lend on a £30 million deal, but no more. It is very difficult to find senior financing today."

While interviewees in last year's survey feared how the refinancing problem would affect banks' ability to undertake new lending, another ugly and intractable problem has since reared its head, only adding to problems of getting access to debt.

Regulation, in the form of Basel III, and government pressure on some key European lenders to real estate to reverse out of the sector have not only tightened the debt markets further, but also promise to choke supply in the future—for how long, no one knows. "There's a regulation race going on to make banks whiter than white, and there is nothing we can do to stop it."

Bankers interviewed summarised the impact of Basel III as "making it very difficult for banks to be aggressive lenders in real estate." "It will require banks to increase margins significantly. If Basel III is going to be introduced as it stands now, liquidity will become terribly expensive." Another added that the consequence of new capital constraints over the next five years will be that "banks will be less willing to provide real estate finance."

Surveys reveal that even though the measures will not officially take effect for quite some time, the industry is already witnessing the effect of Basel III on lenders. As one interviewee noted, "The biggest problem today for the banks is regulation and the administrative load they are under. It will slow them dramatically down. The more the government is involved in a bank, the worse it is. States are trying to put such heavy chains on them that they are completely consumed. It is very hard for them to do new business."

Interviewees fear that a severe consequence for the market will be the withdrawal of German banks, which have

EXHIBIT 1-8

European Commercial Real Estate Debt Maturity Profile

Legend:
- U.K.
- Germany
- Rest of Europe

Euros (Billions) by year: 2011, 2012, 2013, 2014, 2015, 2016, 2017, 2018, 2019, 2020

Sources: CB Richard Ellis; De Montfort University.

Note: As of the end of 2010, €960 billion of debt will be maturing in the next ten years, of which 55 percent is due to mature in the next three years alone.

been key lenders to real estate during the downturn. In 2010, the market witnessed the decision to shut down one bank's international business, tripping anxiety that others could follow. "If German banks exit the market, then what and who [will lend to real estate]?"

"It is bad. It is really bad," one interviewee from a German bank admitted. "Over the last couple of years, liquidity that existed was dependent on the German banks. Basel III has been a big thing, and every bank is being audited on how it allocates capital and what that means under Basel III. Some European banks are being given three years to get to the ratio the regulator wants, but the German regulators are saying, 'No, be there tomorrow.'"

Despite the low-interest-rate environment, interviewees say the cost of debt is likely to be "horrendous." Some see evidence that the price of debt has even risen since June—just months before Basel III was pushed through. "Liquidity will be there, but at a very big cost." "If customers want to increase their LTVs [loan-to-value ratios] on assets, they will have to pay considerably more than they used to," said one banker.

The impact on the real estate market of these long-term changes will be a continuation of a severe bifurcation between those who can obtain debt finance and those who cannot.

In some interviews, it was suggested that business models must be adapted to this new era. "There are those that think financing is a problem. But if you need debt to drive your business model, then you have the wrong model. Those guys that think they need more than 60 percent debt on a deal are in trouble. Too much noise about the need for leverage comes from the property press and seminars and from financially driven people who are trained to be noisy. Their voices should be heard, but their relevance is to be questioned."

The following is how those interviewed analysed the key trends for 2011:

Refinancing woes: There is no debt capital available for refinancing a property with vacancy or which is in need of refurbishment.

Scarce development finance: Development financing is not available, although for the bigger established firms, "at least banks will now open the door and maybe even offer you a chair."

Relationship banking: Banks have developed stringent policies for who they'd like to support going forward. "Although they are seeing a multitude of potential clients, they are only being allowed to support one or two sponsors."

Super prime: Prime office, shopping centres, and hotels will attract finance because whatever happens economically, they will be in demand. "What is the compensation for going off and doing something somewhere else?" asked one banker.

Banks go home: As governments put pressure on banks to support businesses at home, banks will continue to retrench. "Six months ago I would have said it was a short-term thing, but more and more I feel some banks are really retreating from the real estate debt business, and we will see more players disappearing."

Sector plays: "If you want to develop residential or student housing, which are sectors where people feel good about the underlying demand drivers, then you can get debt. But your expectations shouldn't be too high. If you are talking about offices, you better have a pre-lease."

Low LTVs: As long as you are not looking for more than a 50 to 60 percent loan-to-value ratio and provided the amount you are seeking is not too big, loans are possible. "It is more difficult than I was expecting it to be. We will get to the point next year where there is plenty of equity around and no debt."

New Sources of Lending

With traditional sources of real estate finance so constrained, interviewees are hopeful that alternative debt providers will emerge during 2011. "Insurance, pension, sovereign wealth, family offices, REITs [real estate investment trusts], and property companies—they will all have capital. The question is, can they get the debt?"

Drawing encouragement from Bank of China's $800 million refinancing of a Manhattan office tower in 2010 and the leasing of space by two Chinese banks in the City of London, some hope that Chinese banks will be important providers of debt, although some argue that this is wishful thinking.

More widespread is the view that insurance companies—bolstered by Solvency II and in search of higher-yielding assets—will step into the market to undertake senior lending. This is tipped by interviewees as "one of the highlights to watch in 2011." "They will have very good business to do, and we will see more of it appearing." Solvency II, a significant regulatory change for the insurance industry likely to be implemented by the end of 2012, will require European insurance companies to put aside extra capital for certain investments, which will encourage them to undertake property lending as a more efficient use of capital than investing in direct property assets.

Support for the idea that insurance companies will be the saviours of the debt markets range from the bullish to the lukewarm, but most agree that they will stay in the conservative 0 to 65 percent LTV space and are not likely to undertake anything risky such as speculative development lending.

Similarly, interviewees predict that mezzanine financing will be available in the months to come, but there are not as many investors providing it as there should be given the need for it in the market.

A handful of reasons for this were raised by interviewees: mezzanine financing is still too expensive, it is hard to raise capital for mezzanine funds, and the lack of senior lending available makes it difficult for the funds to deploy capital. "We see a few people out there doing it. People recognize that there are opportunities in that space, but I don't think the money has really been raised—not enough to fill the debt gap. I think we are some way away from market saturation."

When asked about the prospect of a return of the European commercial mortgage–backed securities (CMBS) market, interviewees said "CMBS is down but not out. It will be back in time, but in adult form"; "From a marketing point of view, it needs a different name." Others said that if there were a true European CMBS deal in 2011, it would be for a single-borrower deal with a single asset and predictable cash flows.

Mountain of Debt, but No Fire Sale

A "huge problem coming over the hill" was the phrase used in last year's *Emerging Trends Europe* report to describe the mountain of debt that needed to be refinanced. This year, interviewees are still at a loss as to how that issue will be resolved. As one aptly put it, "It is a major problem with no solution in sight."

The debt funding gap—the gap between existing debt and the debt available to replace it—will remain the elephant in the room for 2011, surveys indicate.

DTZ estimates that between 2011 and 2013, the global debt funding gap is €183 billion, and Europe has the biggest exposure to that of 51 percent (€94 billion), followed by Asia Pacific at 29 percent and the United States at 20 percent. (DTZ, *Global Debt Funding Gap Report*, November 2010.) Within Europe, Ireland, Spain, and the U.K. have the biggest problems relative to the size of the market. According to DTZ, loans in continental Europe and the U.K. are traditionally for five years, as opposed to the United States, where they are usually for ten years. This means that loans originated in 2007 will need refinancing in 2012, but they will be secured by properties with values 14 percent lower across the continent and 25 percent lower in the U.K.

But baby steps are being taken to tackle these issues and shift distressed properties into the market. DTZ reports that in the U.K. in 2009, 23 assets were sold totalling €1.76 billion. During the first three quarters of 2010, the number of sales by administrators had already doubled to 47, representing an additional €1 billion of sales.

Interviewees say they are seeing a gradual increase of distressed opportunities coming from U.K. and German banks (the "only proactive banks in Europe"), as well as from the National Asset Management Agency (NAMA) in Ireland, and the pace of that activity is quickening.

"In the last four to six weeks, we have seen properties coming to us from administrations, and there are rumors that there are more coming. We are seeing more in the U.K." "I think we'll see more interesting opportunities from the banks in 2011. They have teams together and have seen a recovery in underlying values and are now prepared to move things

EXHIBIT 1-9

Respondents' Global Real Estate Portfolio by World Region and Year

	2010	2011	In Five Years
Europe	82.8%	81.1%	75.5%
Asia Pacific	9.4%	9.7%	10.8%
United States/Canada	5.1%	5.8%	7.9%
Other	2.7%	3.4%	5.9%

Source: *Emerging Trends in Real Estate Europe 2011* survey.

EXHIBIT 1-10

Cross-Border Investment in Europe by Source, Q1–Q3 2010

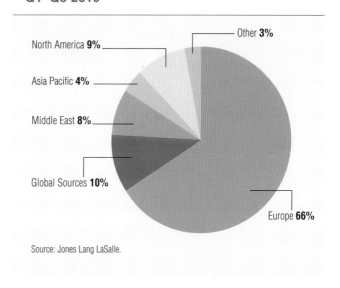

North America **9%**

Asia Pacific **4%**

Middle East **8%**

Global Sources **10%**

Other **3%**

Europe **66%**

Source: Jones Lang LaSalle.

out." Others believe that banks have better resources and are significantly clearer about what they want to achieve than they were a year ago.

Despite these improvements, many interviewees are frustrated by their inability to get access to a greater number of deals at more bargain prices. "It is a bit like watching the grass grow." "A lot of properties are atrophying. The banks won't put more money in. I can help by going to the bank and recapitalising the loan and keeping the borrower in place. When I have tried to do that to date, the banks won't take the pain necessary to make some money, although the gap has narrowed. But they are still loath to write assets down to a level that is sufficient for me."

Some also believe that getting deals out of the banks is a local game. "In Germany, the locals are well tied into the German banks and are starting to be able to cherry pick individual deals where banks do not want to foreclose. But for the British to knock on the door trying to talk about a problem loan portfolio, that is hard."

The bankers interviewed say investors have unrealistic expectations over pricing. "The problem with all banks is that clearing prices for legacy loans are substantially discounted against where banks are carrying those loans, so the losses they have to take on good assets is material. Banks will start moving stuff, but they really can't afford to take capital losses because they will go bust." "If you talk to NAMA or to the banks, you realise that the government won't transact with people seen as exploitative or opportunistic."

It is likely that these irreconcilable points of view will remain for 2011.

Secondary Property

But the real Herculean task for banks is not yet being dealt with, according to interviewees: secondary property—the "ticking time bomb," as some described it.

"We have analysed every investment we made in Europe, and the outcome is staggering: 90 percent of our losses across the world came from very few buildings. A huge portion came from buildings in inferior locations or of inferior quality, or both."

Of the €960 billion of outstanding commercial real estate debt that will mature in Europe over the next ten years, €233 billion is secured against poor-quality assets at high LTVs, according to CB Richard Ellis (see exhibit 1-11). These deals are a major obstacle to the clearing of banks' balance sheets and revival of debt markets, and interviewees foresee this to remain the case in 2011.

The problem for banks is that they are in a catch-22-style scenario, interviewees said. It is impossible to sell these properties without taking a massive loan loss, but also very difficult to hold on to them; the short leases, low-quality assets, and need for capital expenditure means the value is unlikely to rise before the loan matures.

Finding new investors to work with is a difficult task. "If banks have got high-quality assets, they will find a buyer for them. They are out there. But the difficult area is when it is an ill-founded development or ill-quality assets. It is very hard to know what they will do about that." "For the truly obsolete properties that valuers just drove by quickly and hit a value that made the deal work—those deals will struggle more than anyone thought."

Interviewees interested in investing in secondary property in 2011 are looking to do so at severe discounts both because of a lack of debt available, and because they want the price to reflect the risk they are undertaking on the asset. This implies that for these deals to clear, prices will have to come down.

"There is an exciting moment coming later this year [in the U.K.] when all the [spending] cuts come in, unemployment rises, maybe interest rates rise a little bit, and there will be an exciting opportunity. Secondary [properties] will come on the market [and] values will have to fall to a level

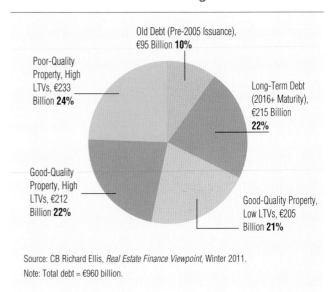

EXHIBIT 1-11
European Commercial Real Estate: Current Profile of Outstanding Debt

Old Debt (Pre-2005 Issuance), €95 Billion **10%**

Poor-Quality Property, High LTVs, €233 Billion **24%**

Long-Term Debt (2016+ Maturity), €215 Billion **22%**

Good-Quality Property, High LTVs, €212 Billion **22%**

Good-Quality Property, Low LTVs, €205 Billion **21%**

Source: CB Richard Ellis, *Real Estate Finance Viewpoint*, Winter 2011.
Note: Total debt = €960 billion.

where you can buy assets with just equity; you will still make a sensible return. The question is who is going to respond. There aren't many secondary players with capital to play with like that."

It looks as though the market will work in investors' favour. Interviewees overwhelmingly anticipate a continued decline of secondary values in 2011, given the shortage of finance. "Unless the banks start lending again—which is very unlikely—the differential between prime and secondary values will continue to widen."

Whereas in 2010 the question was "when is the fire sale?" Europe's real estate industry today is focussed on a different issue. Some had feared that if banks dumped properties on the market, there was a risk of major price reversals. But the concern today is that the pressure of regulation and the conundrum over secondary property will lead to further stagnation in the market.

Could this be a positive development for the industry? A controversial view aired during interviews and worth noting is that debt is out of vogue. Interviewees urge people to rethink their approach to property in the context of this new climate.

"To my mind, we shouldn't have leverage at all. And for the long-term investor, the current difficulty of people getting debt is an absolute dream; it is perfect. It keeps the short-term investors out of the game," said one. Another said, "Value creation and all the skills traditionally valued by those in real estate will be important now. Losses have not been made by real estate professionals; they were made by financial arbitrage. I think if you have a well-placed business and are playing carefully and know what you're doing, you have reasons to be optimistic."

Regulation, Regulation, Regulation

"There is too much pending legislation written by people who don't understand what is going on," said one interviewee. "Am I angst ridden about regulation? Everybody is. There is way too much on the regulation front." Said another, "Everybody is fraught with the regulatory shadow."

Whether it is Solvency II, Basel III, the Alternative Investment Fund Managers Directive (AIFMD), or lease accounting changes, regulators promise to throw more uncertainty at the market in 2011. "A wealth of risk-averse legislation awaits European institutions."

There is hope in some quarters that Solvency II will push insurers into property lending because it is a more efficient way to invest in the market, while others worry that the regulations will deter insurance companies from investing directly or indirectly in real estate. One interviewee even envisioned that in the worst-case scenario, "it could lead to a massive watershed for the German property industry, leading institutional investors to turn away from property,"

The AIFMD was approved by the European Parliament in November and in 2011 will start its committee phases, where the detail will be hammered out to enable its transition into national law of the member states.

Opinions of those interviewed regarding the directive ranged from the livid to the entirely unconcerned. Some fear that smaller fund managers, unable to meet the massive administrative costs, would be pushed out of the business; passing on fees to investors is unlikely to be welcomed by the investors the AIFMD seeks to protect. Others see this as an opportunity to buy defunct firms. Interviewees also predicted that the regulations would introduce high barriers of entry for new firms just as the market desperately needs new blood.

A further source of anxiety is the European Union's efforts to improve transparency and risk management in the market in over-the-counter (OTC) derivatives—including interest rate and currency swaps. Property firms that use interest rate swaps to reduce the risk of movements in interest rates, for example, could be forced by the regulation to put aside collateral for their derivatives transactions in cash.

The E.U. is mainly targeting regulation at financial firms that trade in OTC derivatives. However, it seems set to treat property funds that are caught by the AIFMD in the same way, even though they use derivatives purely for risk management rather than profit.

The British Property Federation has warned that the proposed E.U. rules on derivatives could confront Europe's property industry with a cash call of as much as €64.9 billion if a solution is not found.

Said an interviewee, "It poses a real threat to real estate companies, as interest rate swaps would need to be marked to market on a daily basis, and many companies including ours would simply not have enough cash to cover these margins."

There is hope that regulators will rectify the "outlandish," "nutty" proposals governing derivatives in 2011.

Sustainability

Many innovative strategies may have been lost as the industry shrinks, but the green agenda is not among them. Among interviewee comments: "It is front and centre"; "It has become unavoidable"; and "It is commercial common sense." Sustainability is not such a focus on account of the industry becoming more altruistic after its brush with mortality, but because investing in or developing sustainable buildings is now part and parcel of making safe investment choices.

Sustainability will be connected with high quality, and this is the real change for 2011 and beyond. "Green buildings will undoubtedly become the benchmark in the coming years: a healthier, better-quality product—more attractive and more marketable." Meanwhile, the capital value of nongreen buildings will fall in the future, surveys indicated.

It is the value that tenants now place on green buildings that is driving these changes. Tenants increasingly are looking for ways to drive operating costs lower and for energy-friendly buildings that reinforce their corporate social responsibility missions, people surveyed said. Some reported they had seen evidence of tenants paying more for green assets, but that view was by no means widespread. Developing a more sustainable building was even linked to enabling smoother relationships between real estate firms and planners.

"It is of growing importance—much less from an ecological or altruistic perspective, but economically." "It is one additional factor in defining what is prime and what is not. A building with good green characteristics will stay let versus one that isn't." "Sustainable buildings do not attract higher rents, but they lease in a weak market." "A few years ago it was about how much rental differential there may be. That isn't so much the question today. [The question] is if you have a high-quality building and want to get a certain price, you have no choice but to make it green."

But it is also a crucial part of attracting talent. "Graduates ask just as much about our corporate social responsibility policy as they do about our compensation policy."

Developers (particularly those in the residential sector), government organisations, shareholders, and occupiers are more keyed into sustainability than investors, however.

Fund managers interviewed remain skeptical over the prospect of financial rewards. "I have not seen a model where private equity investors are willing to pay for it and take the lower returns." Their stance was bolstered recently when the U.K.'s Investment Property Databank and K&L Gates released figures showing that sustainable properties have underperformed their less-green counterparts by 400 basis points since the first quarter of 2008.

Real Estate Capital Flows

"In 2011, equity investors will come back to the market, but they will be more and more demanding."

Equity will rule the world in 2011. The European real estate industry is nearly unanimous in its belief that the flow of equity capital into that market will recover. But when it comes to debt, the industry is far less optimistic. The substantial undersupply of debt is expected to continue through 2011 and be worse than in previous years.

"Banks will hold on new loans waiting for their current ones to get out of any potential trouble first," one interviewee said. This opinion is shared by 83.7 percent of those surveyed; they expect real estate debt capital markets to be substantially or moderately undersupplied this year.

Show Me the Money!

"During 2009 and 2010, funds have been retracted from the real estate market, and the money that has been left there has been focused on core investments," noted one interviewee. "However, the availability of equity capital today is enormous and real estate remains an important part of any

well-balanced portfolio, and, therefore, the money will flow back soon." The undersupply of equity indeed appears to be over. In 2010, 62 percent of the respondents rated the real estate equity market as substantially or moderately undersupplied. But skies are blue again in 2011, and the percentage of pessimists has fallen to 47 percent.

This optimism, however, varies among the different type of respondents. Private funds, especially, tend to be the most pessimistic when it comes to the outlook of the equity

EXHIBIT 2-1

Real Estate Equity Capital Market Balance Prospects for 2011

Moderately Undersupplied **35.3%**   Moderately Oversupplied **25.0%**

Substantially Undersupplied **11.7%**   In Balance **23.7%**   Substantially Oversupplied **4.3%**

Source: *Emerging Trends in Real Estate Europe 2011* survey.

EXHIBIT 2-2

Perspectives on Real Estate Equity Capital Market Balance Prospects for 2011, by Firm Type

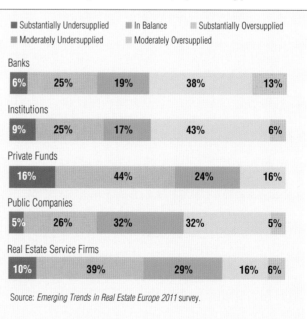

■ Substantially Undersupplied   ■ In Balance   ▨ Substantially Oversupplied
■ Moderately Undersupplied   ▨ Moderately Oversupplied

Banks
6%   25%   19%   38%   13%

Institutions
9%   25%   17%   43%   6%

Private Funds
16%   44%   24%   16%

Public Companies
5%   26%   32%   32%   5%

Real Estate Service Firms
10%   39%   29%   16%   6%

Source: *Emerging Trends in Real Estate Europe 2011* survey.

EXHIBIT 2-3
Real Estate Debt Capital Market Balance Prospects for 2011

Moderately Undersupplied **38.7%**　Moderately Oversupplied **3.0%**

Substantially Undersupplied **45.0%**　In Balance **12.0%**

Substantially Oversupplied **1.3%**

Source: *Emerging Trends in Real Estate Europe 2011* survey.

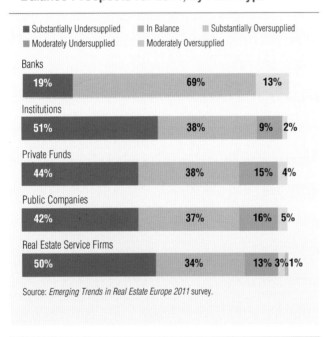

EXHIBIT 2-4
Perspectives on Real Estate Debt Capital Market Balance Prospects for 2011, by Firm Type

- Substantially Undersupplied
- In Balance
- Substantially Oversupplied
- Moderately Undersupplied
- Moderately Oversupplied

Banks
19% | 69% | 13%

Institutions
51% | 38% | 9% | 2%

Private Funds
44% | 38% | 15% | 4%

Public Companies
42% | 37% | 16% | 5%

Real Estate Service Firms
50% | 34% | 13% | 3% | 1%

Source: *Emerging Trends in Real Estate Europe 2011* survey.

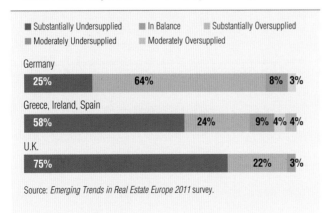

EXHIBIT 2-5
Perspectives on Real Estate Debt Capital Market Balance Prospects for 2011, by Country

- Substantially Undersupplied
- In Balance
- Substantially Oversupplied
- Moderately Undersupplied
- Moderately Oversupplied

Germany
25% | 64% | 8% | 3%

Greece, Ireland, Spain
58% | 24% | 9% | 4% | 4%

U.K.
75% | 22% | 3%

Source: *Emerging Trends in Real Estate Europe 2011* survey.

market in 2011: 60.2 percent of private funds consider the equity market undersupplied. "Real estate investments in Europe will not grow, as investors seek low risk and high profits in countries like Brazil, Turkey, India, and China," one interviewee said.

But among the publicly listed property companies, spirits are high again. Here, less than 32 percent of the respondents expect an undersupplied real estate equity market in Europe during 2011. "The recovery after the crisis is leading to good business opportunities over the next five years. We established a basis for participation in the improving markets in the years 2009–2010, and we expect investors to line up soon." Especially when the expectations on equity flows are benchmarked to prospects for the debt market, the European real estate equity outlook is strong indeed.

As for the real estate debt market, the pessimism is shown in exhibit 2-3. The vast majority of those surveyed have little faith that the availability of debt will recover. Whereas in 2008, 79.5 percent of the respondents considered the real estate debt market to be undersupplied, that percentage now has risen further to a staggering 83.7 percent. "Debt providers seem to recover more slowly than equity providers. The reason for this is likely to be the fact that these investors are still faced with a large volume of instruments of low recoverability, the value of which has not yet been adjusted. Although it is to be expected that more debt capital will be available at acceptable conditions as the economy recovers, the lack of available credit will slow down real estate developments for the time being."

This consensus on the bleak outlook on debt availability is strong. The surveyed bankers turned out to be milder in their assessment, preferring to label the real estate debt market moderately rather than substantially undersupplied. Other actors in the European real estate industry are more convinced that the undersupply will be substantial. Also, a comparison of opinions on the debt market across nations reveals interesting differences. Respondents from the U.K. have been the most negative about the 2011 supply of debt. In fact, expectations in the U.K. on debt availability are even worse than those in markets like Greece, Ireland, and Spain. In Germany, the vast majority shares this pessimism, but thinks of it in more moderate terms.

Equity: Coming Your Way

Investors are ready to take on real estate investments again. An examination of the origins of equity capital expected to flow into the European real estate industry reveals some mild shifts. Overall, Europe is expected to remain rather constant as a supply of equity funds; increased flows are expected from countries with relatively strong economies like Germany and the Netherlands, and reduced flows are anticipated from Spain and Italy. Most of the increase in fund flows is expected from other parts

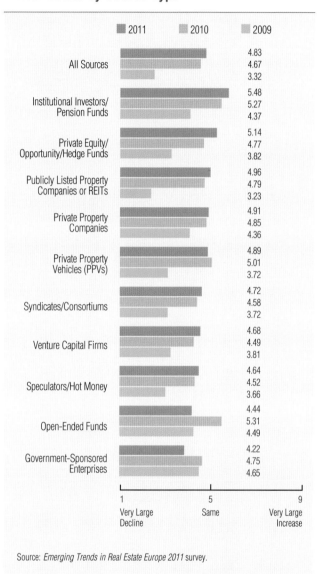

EXHIBIT 2-6

Change in Availability of Equity Capital for Real Estate by Source Location

■ 2011   ■ 2010   ■ 2009

Source	2011	2010	2009
Asia Pacific	6.29	5.68	4.55
Middle East	5.53	5.39	5.39
Germany	5.49	5.40	4.15
United States/Canada	5.29	5.02	3.44
U.K.	4.99	5.11	3.27
France	4.98	5.00	3.74
Europe	4.98	4.98	3.72
Netherlands	4.87	4.79	3.84
Italy	3.98	4.29	3.21
Spain	3.38	3.63	2.59

1 Very Large Decline   5 Same   9 Very Large Increase

Source: *Emerging Trends in Real Estate Europe 2011* survey.

EXHIBIT 2-7

Change in Availability of Equity Capital for Real Estate by Source Type

■ 2011   ■ 2010   ■ 2009

Source	2011	2010	2009
All Sources	4.83	4.67	3.32
Institutional Investors/Pension Funds	5.48	5.27	4.37
Private Equity/Opportunity/Hedge Funds	5.14	4.77	3.82
Publicly Listed Property Companies or REITs	4.96	4.79	3.23
Private Property Companies	4.91	4.85	4.36
Private Property Vehicles (PPVs)	4.89	5.01	3.72
Syndicates/Consortiums	4.72	4.58	3.72
Venture Capital Firms	4.68	4.49	3.81
Speculators/Hot Money	4.64	4.52	3.66
Open-Ended Funds	4.44	5.31	4.49
Government-Sponsored Enterprises	4.22	4.75	4.65

1 Very Large Decline   5 Same   9 Very Large Increase

Source: *Emerging Trends in Real Estate Europe 2011* survey.

of the globe; especially, Asian equity is expected to gain importance during 2011.

"Source markets such as Russia, China, and Arab/Middle East countries are becoming increasingly more important," one interviewee said. "To this end, emphasis should be towards a more sophisticated real estate product 'packaged' with tailor-made service offerings so as to best tap these source markets."

When asked for the source type of fresh real estate equity, the 2011 survey respondents said they expect pension funds, private equity, and real estate investment trusts to be standing first in line. And the importance of these three types of investors is expected to expand at the highest rate. "Equity capital will come from many different sources. REITs and publicly listed vehicles can recapitalize themselves with rights issues. Listed vehicles, sovereign wealth funds, and pension funds are looking for more, but there is not much stock of that available currently. Active managers that can take secondary stock and fix it up to a stabilized asset will have a lot of opportunities to make returns." A remarkable change is the expected drop in the appetite of open-ended funds, especially compared with a year ago when these funds were expected to become the winners of 2010. "The money was just dropping in." But for 2011, this view has changed. "For the open-ended funds, we'd expect there to be a dichotomy. Some will remain

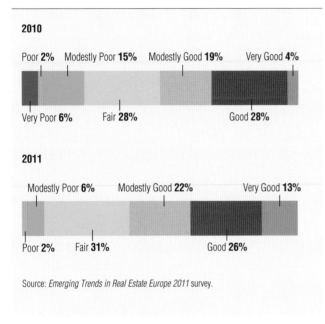

EXHIBIT 2-8
Expected Business Profitability—Institutions

2010

Poor **2%** Modestly Poor **15%** Modestly Good **19%** Very Good **4%**

Very Poor **6%** Fair **28%** Good **28%**

2011

Modestly Poor **6%** Modestly Good **22%** Very Good **13%**

Poor **2%** Fair **31%** Good **26%**

Source: *Emerging Trends in Real Estate Europe 2011* survey.

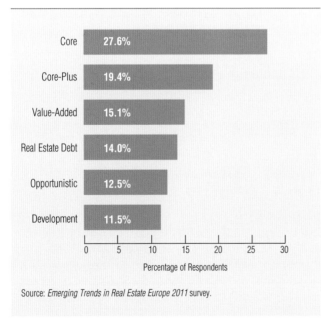

EXHIBIT 2-9
Where Would Institutional Money Flow?

Category	Percentage
Core	27.6%
Core-Plus	19.4%
Value-Added	15.1%
Real Estate Debt	14.0%
Opportunistic	12.5%
Development	11.5%

Percentage of Respondents

Source: *Emerging Trends in Real Estate Europe 2011* survey.

active in the market; they are not affected at all. They will see further inflow of funds, while others are actually closed and some funds are being liquidated." A detailed discussion of what the survey found regarding these four types of equity provider follows.

Institutions Can See Clearly Now

The surveyed institutional investors have regained their confidence in the outlook of the real estate investment industry. When asked for their opinion on expected business profitability, thumbs went up across the board. The various shades of optimism today account for 61.2 percent of the total, and only 8.1 percent still expect real estate performance to be poor during the next year.

"Institutional interest in real estate as an 'alternative investment' will increase," one person interviewed said. "We will continue to offer funds who themselves will be in the alternative space and which will look to benefit from the exit opportunities embedded."

The institutions were asked where in the real estate industry they would invest money, if they had a substantial amount of capital to invest. Core is still king, as exhibit 2-9 shows. Institutions are reluctant to accept the risks faced by opportunistic funds and are not eager to put their money in real estate development ventures. "We are mostly looking for core properties—hands-on asset management," one interviewee said. Or, as another said, "When thinking of the future, we think of less liquidity, lower LTVs, and fewer speculative developments. We will spend more effort and energy on asset management, value creation, and maintaining current relationships rather than depending upon nonorganic growth."

State Capitalists

A year ago, sovereign wealth funds (SWFs) were considered big beasts that were rethinking their strategies. During 2010 they seemed to have made up their mind about real estate. "Sovereign wealth funds will be a huge source giving a carte blanche for real estate funds," an interviewee said. Though real estate has ranked in the top ten of the Sovereign Wealth Fund Institute's Consensus Demand Meter, it had been struggling at position number nine. Now, though, the tide has turned, and today real estate is hot again among SWFs and ranks high in popularity polls (see exhibit 2-10).

As a group, SWFs have well over €3.5 trillion of assets under management—funds that are scattered across a vast variety of funds. Besides well-known giants like the Abu Dhabi Investment Authority, which has been around since 1976 and currently manages a portfolio of well over €500 billion, new kids on the block also appear—for instance, the Sovereign Fund of Brazil, which manages €8 billion. In

EXHIBIT 2-10
Sovereign Wealth Funds Consensus Demand Meter, Q4 2010

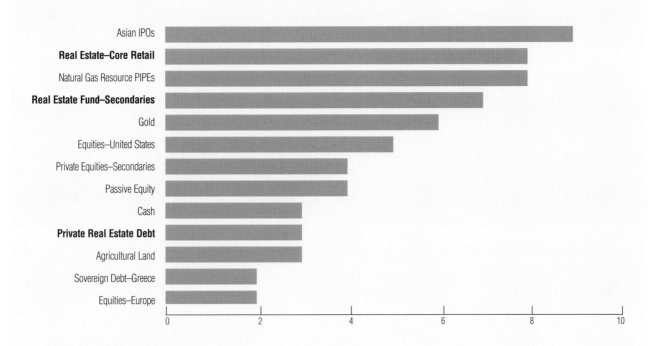

Source: Sovereign Wealth Fund Institute, December 2010.

Note: The Consensus Demand Meter tracks what sovereign wealth funds are demanding over the next three quarters on a scale of 10 (attractive to a majority or large portion of SWFs) to 1 (SWFs will most likely try to lower exposure).

EXHIBIT 2-11
Sovereign Wealth Funds by Funding Source

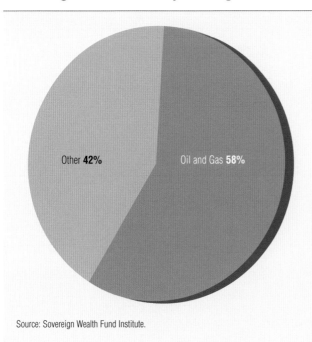

Source: Sovereign Wealth Fund Institute.

EXHIBIT 2-12
Sovereign Wealth Funds by Region

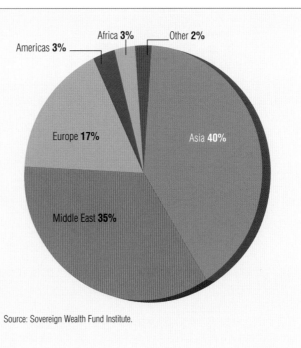

Source: Sovereign Wealth Fund Institute.

58 percent of cases, oil and gas revenues are the source of funding, and 75 percent of the SWFs originate in either Asia or the Middle East. The evolution of the SWF industry has been swift. Transparency concerning portfolio structure, investment policies, and origins of wealth is fueled by novel rating initiatives.

Private Equity

The position of private equity funds in 2011 is interesting. When survey respondents were asked about the sources of equity, they said little money is expected to flow from private and open-ended funds. But when operators of these private equity funds themselves were asked for their take on the future profitability of the business, they turned out to be almost as optimistic as institutional investors. For 2011, 49.7 percent of all open-ended funds in the *Emerging Trends Europe* survey expect real estate profits to be modestly good or better. For 2010, the portion was less than 30 percent, representing an impressive boost in confidence among this type of equity investor in the past year.

EXHIBIT 2-14
Expected Business Profitability—Private Equity Funds

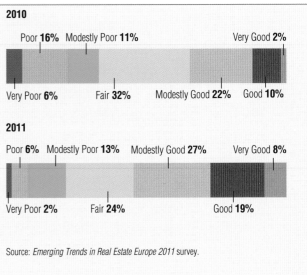

2010

Poor **16%**   Modestly Poor **11%**   Very Good **2%**

Very Poor **6%**   Fair **32%**   Modestly Good **22%**   Good **10%**

2011

Poor **6%**   Modestly Poor **13%**   Modestly Good **27%**   Very Good **8%**

Very Poor **2%**   Fair **24%**   Good **19%**

Source: *Emerging Trends in Real Estate Europe 2011* survey.

EXHIBIT 2-13
Growth of Private Property Vehicles in Europe

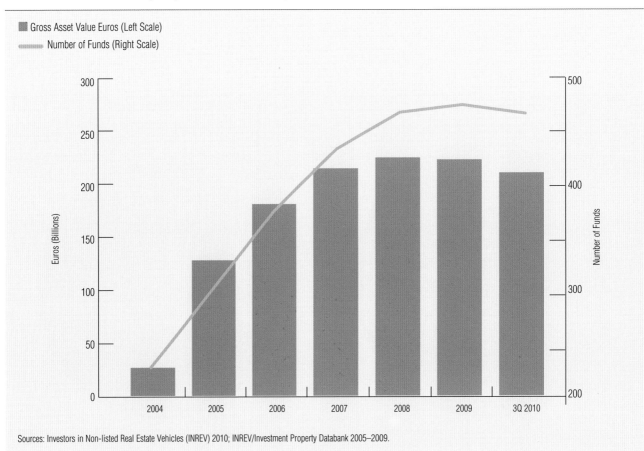

■ Gross Asset Value Euros (Left Scale)
▬▬ Number of Funds (Right Scale)

Sources: Investors in Non-listed Real Estate Vehicles (INREV) 2010; INREV/Investment Property Databank 2005–2009.

This apparent discrepancy between confidence among these investors and low expectations in the real estate industry concerning private equity flows may perhaps be best explained by the sudden halt in growth of the private property vehicle market that started in 2008 and progressed during 2010. In fact, for the first time in many years, the European private equity real estate market has declined both in number of existing fund companies and gross asset values. This may feed into the perception in the real estate investment industry that equity flows from private equity during 2011 will be modest at best.

REITs

REITs had a good year in 2010. After fierce declines during 2007 and 2008 and a mild recovery in 2009, 2010 was the year of the real bounce back. Price indices for Sweden and Switzerland have rebounded to pre-crisis levels. The future of REIT performance also appears to be positive.

"REITs and listed property companies have a competitive advantage due to their lower cost of capital and access to public equity and debt capital markets," one

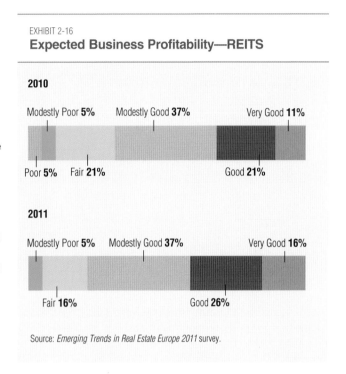

EXHIBIT 2-16
Expected Business Profitability—REITS

2010

Modestly Poor **5%** Modestly Good **37%** Very Good **11%**

Poor **5%** Fair **21%** Good **21%**

2011

Modestly Poor **5%** Modestly Good **37%** Very Good **16%**

Fair **16%** Good **26%**

Source: *Emerging Trends in Real Estate Europe 2011* survey.

EXHIBIT 2-15
EPRA/NAREIT Real Estate Stock Price Indices

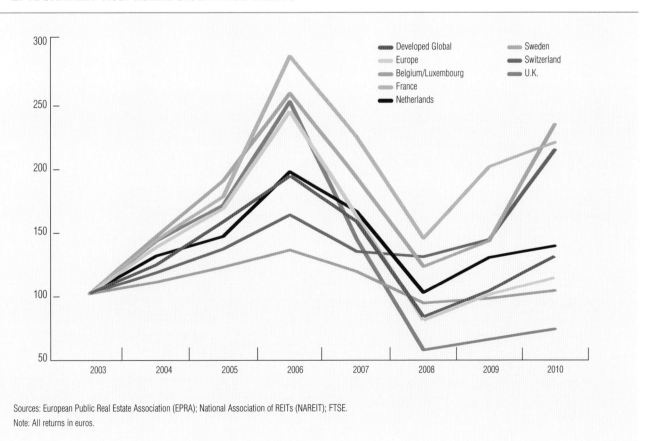

Developed Global
Europe
Belgium/Luxembourg
France
Netherlands
Sweden
Switzerland
U.K.

Sources: European Public Real Estate Association (EPRA); National Association of REITs (NAREIT); FTSE.
Note: All returns in euros.

interviewee noted. Just 5.1 percent of the REIT respondents surveyed were expecting poor profitability for 2011; 64.2 percent are expecting 2011 profitability to be modestly good or better.

But besides these prosperous profits, survey respondents also expect new waves of corporate dynamics among REITs. "The REIT industry will consolidate into larger conglomerates," one interviewee said. "The relevant measure is to be prepared for takeovers; it's better playing the active than the passive role." While the real estate industry is keeping a sharp eye on REITs as suppliers of equity, REITs may well be very busy tracking each other for different reasons.

Debt: Playing by the New Rules

"There is not a lot of debt capital out there. The banks should be more willing to lend and charge more for it if they feel the need in order that they cover their risks and get healthy again to facilitate normal lending activities in the future." This quote from one of the interviewees summarizes the 2011 sentiments regarding debt. This year is expected to be yet another in which debt is rationed. "2011 is not anticipated to be a promising year for new debt issues in the market. All major debt sources have plenty of issues to resolve, a significant percentage of

existing debt expires, and refinancing will be of main concern rather than additional debt issues."

Loan recovery is still dominating the scene, and banks are not keen on going back to business as usual. In fact, 'usual' is currently being redefined. "Banks are quite slow to start lending again due to ratios. German, U.K., and Irish banks are no longer in the same situation to act in the same capacity. There are some players that weathered the storm, like French banks. New players like Chinese banks are active in London and Paris."

The standards are being adjusted and, as was the case in the years before this adjustment, the standards are expected to be strict. Of the *Emerging Trends Europe* interviewees, 69.1 percent expect debt underwriting standards to become more rigorous, whereas only 55.6 percent expect equity underwriting to be more rigorous.

EXHIBIT 2-19
Change in Availability of Debt Capital for Real Estate

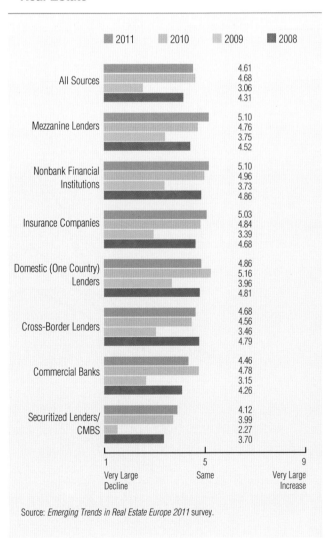

Source: *Emerging Trends in Real Estate Europe 2011* survey.

EXHIBIT 2-17
Debt Underwriting Standards Prospects for 2011

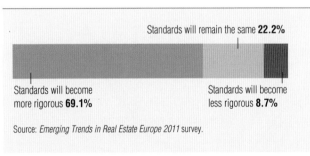

Standards will remain the same **22.2%**

Standards will become more rigorous **69.1%**

Standards will become less rigorous **8.7%**

Source: *Emerging Trends in Real Estate Europe 2011* survey.

EXHIBIT 2-18
Equity Underwriting Standards Prospects for 2011

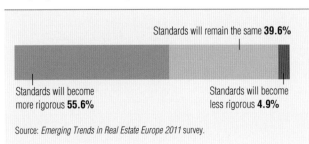

Standards will remain the same **39.6%**

Standards will become more rigorous **55.6%**

Standards will become less rigorous **4.9%**

Source: *Emerging Trends in Real Estate Europe 2011* survey.

Debt Facilitators

An important matter when it comes to debt availability is the question of who will supply the debt. In interviews, survey participants provided very specific forecasts. "Banks are coming back, but at lower LTV ratios and higher margins," one interviewee said. "CMBS will come back at the highest quality in 2011, but it's a slow process. We will see a new type of lender like insurance companies entering the space, as this is a good way to get some yielding assets in their portfolios. Mezzanine lenders in the form of private funds are small, as there is no demand for high leverage at the moment." An aggregation of the expectations on debt facilitators yields the results shown in exhibit 2-19.

In many ways, the results from the survey in this area are very similar to those of a year ago. In 2010, respondents were expecting no change in the status quo regarding both the overall availability of debt and the breakdown of debt sources. This year, it seems that not a lot has changed. But this stable opinion applies mostly to the consensus. Individual opinions on debt availability vary quite a lot. "Spreads have been reducing since the beginning of the crisis," one person interviewed said. "Access

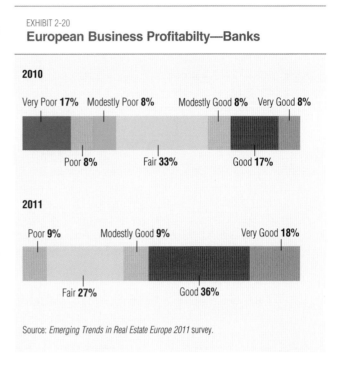

EXHIBIT 2-20
European Business Profitabilty—Banks

Source: *Emerging Trends in Real Estate Europe 2011* survey.

EXHIBIT 2-21
CMBS Issuance

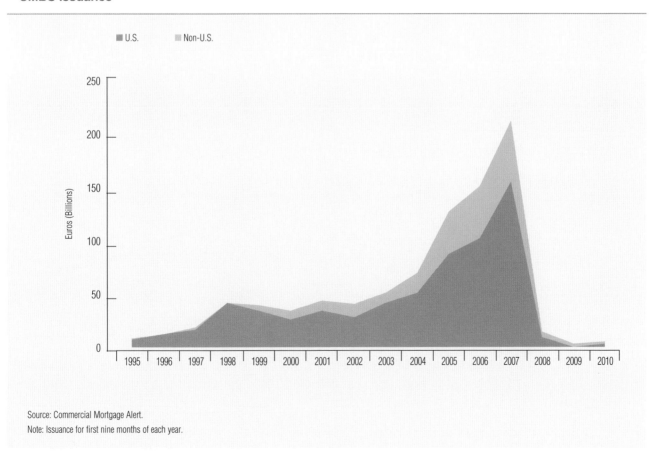

Source: Commercial Mortgage Alert.
Note: Issuance for first nine months of each year.

to debt capital is becoming noticeably easier, but high-volume credits are still scarce to receive only with LTV ratios below 70 percent and high spreads. CMBS markets are crunched since 2007. Huge CMBS volumes are going to be due from 2013. Established market standard is repayment during contract period. So we expect reluctance of banks to make debt available."

But there is also hope. When bankers alone are questioned regarding their confidence, they see a light at the end of the tunnel and they are sure it is not a train coming their way. Though no banks appear sure, their level of optimism has doubled. A year ago, 33.3 percent of the bankers surveyed were expecting business profitability to be good or better. This year, 63.6 percent express this optimism, indicating that confidence among bankers is gaining momentum. At the same time, the real estate industry at large is less convinced about the bankers' willingness to return to business. "New opportunities are emerging for commercial banks in term of investments in particular types of products/services," an interviewee said. "Due to the current turmoil among the financial markets, these commercial banks are downsizing the number of the loans, showing a particular attention to the stability and the financial conditions of the counterparties. The number of banks financing the [real estate] sector is very limited; thus, an increase of banks acting in this sector would result in new lending."

CMBS: Life after Death

"Commercial banks are the only debt capital source in our market," one interviewee said. "CMBS is dead." A year ago, respondents were expecting the CMBS sector to resuscitate during 2010, but the statistics prove otherwise. The evolution of CMBS issuances over the past 15 years, plotted in exhibit 2-21, indicates that this industry has fallen off a cliff. Since 2008, issuances have dropped 95 percent, and 2010 has not offered a lot of market evidence that signals recovery in Europe. "CMBS is dead, in my opinion, because of the low transparency of the ownership and inflexibility for a borrower," said one interviewee. Said another, "The CMBS market won't come back in 2011, and further on we don't really see any signs of revival."

But this gloom is not shared by all those interviewed. "During 2011, banks will further suffer, while the CMBS market will come back alive," one interviewee said. A few respondents are certain there is life after death for the CMBS market. These signals of hope are also noted in the financial markets. The CMBS spread has been steadily declining, which implies that the restored confidence is present not only among some of the survey respondents, but also is already driving down the price of risk. In the United States, the CMBS market is picking up the pieces. About $2.4 billion of U.S. CMBS was packaged and sold in the first half of 2010, up from

EXHIBIT 2-22
Ten-Year, AAA CMBS Spreads over Swap Rate

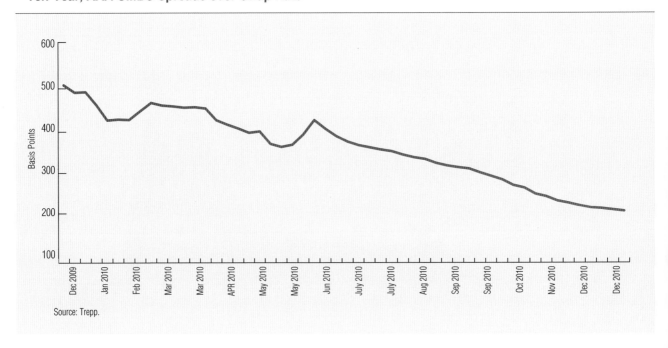

Source: Trepp.

$638.5 million a year earlier, including the rebirth of the multiloan deals key to expanding credit to property buyers. Moreover, between the start of 2011 and the end of 2013, about $150 billion of U.S. CMBS falls due for refinance, compared with $30 billion in Europe. Although one-fifth the size, Europe's CMBS refinancing task may prove a bigger challenge because of inherent structural quirks: the European CMBS market is much younger and did not have a chance to develop many of the strengths of the U.S. product before the downturn.

Derivatives

The young market of European property derivatives struggled during 2010. Trading volumes declined, and a lot of the initial momentum appears to be lost. But here also, optimism among survey respondents remains vivid. "One development that the current crisis may inspire/enhance is the development of real estate derivatives in order to make it possible to trade real estate risk without having to shift actual real estate around," one interviewee said. "The real estate market is relatively old-fashioned when compared to other financial markets. Just take a look at the appraisal market where a simple capitalization of first year's NOI [net operating income] is the predominant technique. Only slowly is DCF [discounted cash flow] modeling entering the market." Patience is required, apparently, because there is little doubt about the value of derivatives as a trading tool.

The market also struggles with other important factors that slow the evolution of the property derivatives market. Initial obstacles persist, like scarce liquidity, settlement risk, and the frequency of the revaluations that underlie the principal indices. The increased focus on risk management in this postcrisis era could fuel market growth in the years to come. However, as one of the interviewees stated, "Derivatives will only play a role in markets where they comply with regulatory requirements of institutional investors." With Solvency II and Basel III—updated banking and insurance industry regulations, respectively—on the horizon, new challenges lie ahead.

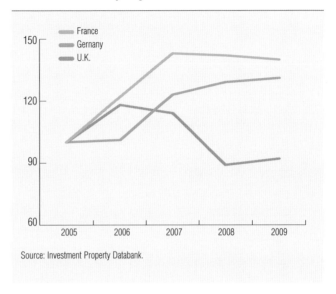

EXHIBIT 2-23
IPD Annual Property Total Return Index

Source: Investment Property Databank.

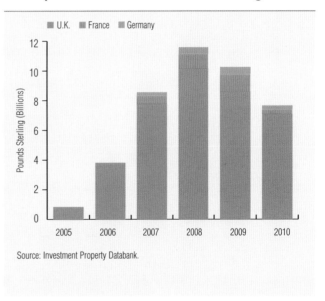

EXHIBIT 2-24
European Real Estate Derivatives Trading Volume

Source: Investment Property Databank.

Markets to Watch

"Munich once again holds the top spot for performance of existing investments."

Last year's *Emerging Trends Europe* report identified a shift in attitude among survey respondents. After a very gloomy prognosis for 2009, interviewees for the 2010 report were showing signs of cautious optimism. In the 2009 report, investment and development prospects were expected to decline across the board: no city showed improvement in either category. For the 2010 report, sentiment regarding investment prospects stabilised, and though the

attitude toward development continued to decline, the drop was less dramatic than that seen in the 2009 report. This year, sentiment toward both investment and development has improved measurably for the first time since 2007.

Many respondents expected some of the key themes from 2009 to continue into 2010—which, indeed, was the case—and the consensus now is that economic recovery will be a long, slow haul well into 2011. Last year was not

---

EXHIBIT 3-1
Average City Prospect Ratings

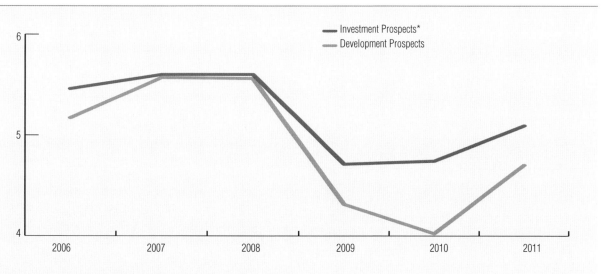

4 = modestly poor, 5 = fair, 6 = modestly good, 7 = good.

Source: *Emerging Trends in Real Estate Europe* surveys.

*Investment prospects are the average of scores for existing property performance and new property acquistions in exhibits 3-2 and 3-3.

the economic disaster that some interviewees for the 2010 report had anticipated; Europe did not slide back into recession. As the slow recovery proceeds, the optimism of respondents varies, but few anticipate anything but modest economic growth in Europe. Said one interviewee, "Europe is the sick man of the world." There is cautious optimism about the German economy, and German respondents are generally more optimistic than others about the prospects for Europe as a whole. However, the broad concern about the state of the European economy remains a key theme. At the other end of the spectrum, there is broad consensus that there is little positive to be said about Athens and Dublin, which are resolutely at the bottom of the table in all three categories rated—existing property performance, new property acquisition, and development.

The general view is that yield compression is over and that in a broadly stagnant economy, general rental growth is also unlikely. In this challenging environment, successful investment will be very asset specific. Strong asset management skills will be the route to achieving returns, rather than picking cities that will outperform. This has a significant impact on the overall survey responses: there is a widespread view that selecting individual cities is not the appropriate approach. One survey respondent described it as "pointless. The answer is stock selection, not markets or cities. All markets have opportunities at the right price."

In particular, it is clear from the survey responses that there is a strong focus on assets that yield cash flow and income. However, the broad consensus that was apparent for 2010 has broken down this year. For 2010, there was a common theme, with investors looking for "plain-vanilla real estate investments that everybody understands"—core and core-plus, "high-quality assets already rented to very good tenants and based in the best central locations" in "the deeper, liquid markets: the U.K., France, and Germany." However, there was a concern that a lot of money was chasing the same assets and that this would push up prices in the more desirable markets. A number of survey respondents suggest that this concern was justified. "London is too expensive and has been for a little while," commented one interviewee. "Paris has now also become too expensive."

The result is that consensus has broken down as to where income can be found. Last year, *Emerging Trends Europe* reported that the "view that performance will be highly dependent on managing the fundamentals and very specific to the individual asset has made many respondents nervous about ranking cities—there is a widespread belief that the quality of the tenant is more important than the city or asset type." This view has this year more strongly manifested itself in the survey responses. Respondents are more reluctant this year than in previous years to express a view on individual cities. Twenty percent of respondents did not rate any cities. An additional 20 percent rated only one city. The number of respondents rating a broad range of cities

was low compared with responses in previous years: only 10 percent of respondents rated more than half the 27 cities in the survey. For any individual city, the percentage of respondents rating it ranged from 10 to 30 percent. When considering the precise relative ranking of cities, readers should take this into account. Survey respondents and interviewees also have been reluctant to provide comments on individual cities in which they invest.

Existing Property Performance

Most respondents comment that 2010 was a year that performed in line with expectations—a year of stability following the dramatic action of 2009. Many said that for their existing portfolios, 2010 was a year of stabilisation in terms of both valuations and the occupier side of the equation. One interviewee in this year's survey described 2010 as "very quiet. The year 2009 was more radical—both organisationally and in terms of portfolio. Both were adjusted in 2009; 2010 was a year of stabilisation." Another commented, "During the last 12 months, the valuations of our real estate have remained stable. Vacancy has grown, but not significantly."

Even where investors have suffered from legacy issues, the pain has been muted by the fact the situation was more or less anticipated. One interviewee noted, "The company had to sell different buildings to obtain some liquidity. However, this bad performance is not as obvious compared to last year because the company had already made major provisions in 2009." This has also fed through into disposal behaviour, with several interviewees reporting that they were able to realise a profit in 2010 by disposing of assets that they had previously written down in 2009. Such disposals are expected to continue into 2011.

There is a clear focus on asset management to maintain the value of existing assets. Several respondents note that they are investing in existing assets to make them more attractive to tenants, and that they are increasing maintenance and capital expenditures.

Although interviewees are generally confident that broad stability will continue into 2011, some areas of concern exist. The fragile economic state of Europe in general could put pressure on tenants. There is a particular concern regarding what a number of respondents refer to as "peripheral Europe"; for example, as one interviewee noted, "Peripheral Europe has issues: Portugal, Spain, Ireland, Greece, and Italy need employment growth in order to further sustain recovery."

The other big concern for some respondents with existing property portfolios is for those with debt due for refinancing. Stabilisation of values and income means that few respondents cite covenant breaches as an immediate concern. However, for those affected, there is a concern about debt maturing in 2011 and even more concern about

EXHIBIT 3-2
City Investment Prospects: Existing Property Performance

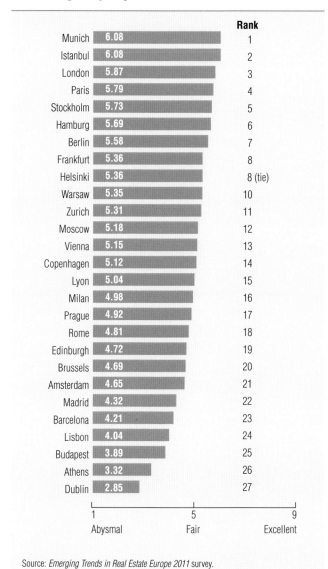

City	Value	Rank
Munich	6.08	1
Istanbul	6.08	2
London	5.87	3
Paris	5.79	4
Stockholm	5.73	5
Hamburg	5.69	6
Berlin	5.58	7
Frankfurt	5.36	8
Helsinki	5.36	8 (tie)
Warsaw	5.35	10
Zurich	5.31	11
Moscow	5.18	12
Vienna	5.15	13
Copenhagen	5.12	14
Lyon	5.04	15
Milan	4.98	16
Prague	4.92	17
Rome	4.81	18
Edinburgh	4.72	19
Brussels	4.69	20
Amsterdam	4.65	21
Madrid	4.32	22
Barcelona	4.21	23
Lisbon	4.04	24
Budapest	3.89	25
Athens	3.32	26
Dublin	2.85	27

1 — Abysmal 5 — Fair 9 — Excellent

Source: *Emerging Trends in Real Estate Europe 2011* survey.

2012. As one interviewee commented, "Refinancing will be the main issue—both the increase in interest cost, but also pressure by banks for a lower LTV ratio will make refinancing discussions particularly difficult." For some respondents, the focus has been on holding off negative consequences. "We were buying time in terms of having finance extended," one commented. Another respondent graphically describes the approach as "delay and pray." Whilst the refinancing challenge is a major concern for those with existing leveraged portfolios, for those looking to invest, this potentially represents an opportunity.

New Property Acquisitions

Though, as noted, the general view is that "the answer is stock selection, not markets or cities," it is also clear from the interviews that this approach is proving difficult to put into practice. Many respondents commented on the difficulty of finding opportunities to deploy capital. Typical comments included, "Currently, the biggest issue is to find attractive assets to invest in," and, "The biggest challenge is to find 'good' new investments—i.e., core assets in top locations with strong tenants." In a market where stock selection and asset management are widely held to be the essential skills, it is perhaps concerning that survey respondents do not generally expect new investments to perform materially better than existing investments, and, in the cases of offices, expect them to perform worse.

EXHIBIT 3-3
City Investment Opportunities: New Property Acquisitions

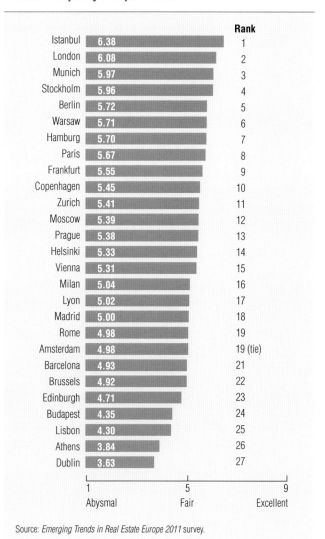

City	Value	Rank
Istanbul	6.38	1
London	6.08	2
Munich	5.97	3
Stockholm	5.96	4
Berlin	5.72	5
Warsaw	5.71	6
Hamburg	5.70	7
Paris	5.67	8
Frankfurt	5.55	9
Copenhagen	5.45	10
Zurich	5.41	11
Moscow	5.39	12
Prague	5.38	13
Helsinki	5.33	14
Vienna	5.31	15
Milan	5.04	16
Lyon	5.02	17
Madrid	5.00	18
Rome	4.98	19
Amsterdam	4.98	19 (tie)
Barcelona	4.93	21
Brussels	4.92	22
Edinburgh	4.71	23
Budapest	4.35	24
Lisbon	4.30	25
Athens	3.84	26
Dublin	3.63	27

1 — Abysmal 5 — Fair 9 — Excellent

Source: *Emerging Trends in Real Estate Europe 2011* survey.

Many interviewees noted that lenders were becoming less enthusiastic in the second half of 2010, with LTV ratios dropping and pricing rising. This has a consequential impact on the optimism of those looking to make acquisitions: those who buy with little or no gearing are generally more optimistic about 2011 than the more highly geared investors.

The 2010 report observed that the key issue across Europe was the availability of assets to acquire and the lack of pressure on sellers to sell. Views differed as to whether the banks would be the trigger of extensive disposals. Last year turned out not to be the one in which lenders were the catalyst for activity, and the consensus of interviewees appears to be that this will remain the case for 2011. Looking out further, interviewees expect the refinancing bubble to be a greater driver of transactions for 2012 and beyond.

It is also worth remembering as a final thought regarding new asset acquisitions that attitudes vary on what constitutes a good asset. In the current risk-averse environment, many low-risk investors cite stability as a key attractive feature. For others, "The most volatile cities are the best to invest in at the bottom of the market. Buy London and Frankfurt at the bottom of the market. Even now they are good bets."

Development

Although the majority of respondents remain focused on acquisitions of new assets, the signs of recovery in sentiment for development identified in the 2010 report have continued to strengthen this year. Some respondents expressed concern over banks' lack of enthusiasm for lending against development projects and that this may be a long-term obstacle to development. Some see this as an opportunity because it may reduce competition. Others are concerned that overreliance on development may leave them exposed to an uncertain future. "We have been known as a developer, and that has changed significantly," one said. "We are changing from being a developer to an acquirer, too. We are keen on expanding as an investment manager."

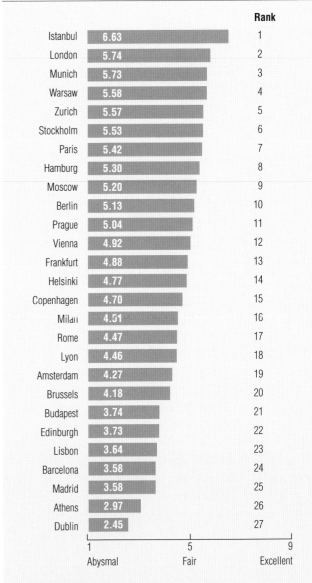

EXHIBIT 3-4
City Development Prospects

City	Score	Rank
Istanbul	6.63	1
London	5.74	2
Munich	5.73	3
Warsaw	5.58	4
Zurich	5.57	5
Stockholm	5.53	6
Paris	5.42	7
Hamburg	5.30	8
Moscow	5.20	9
Berlin	5.13	10
Prague	5.04	11
Vienna	4.92	12
Frankfurt	4.88	13
Helsinki	4.77	14
Copenhagen	4.70	15
Milan	4.51	16
Rome	4.47	17
Lyon	4.46	18
Amsterdam	4.27	19
Brussels	4.18	20
Budapest	3.74	21
Edinburgh	3.73	22
Lisbon	3.64	23
Barcelona	3.58	24
Madrid	3.58	25
Athens	2.97	26
Dublin	2.45	27

1 — Abysmal   5 — Fair   9 — Excellent

Source: *Emerging Trends in Real Estate Europe 2011* survey.

EXHIBIT 3-5
Leading European City Investment Prospects

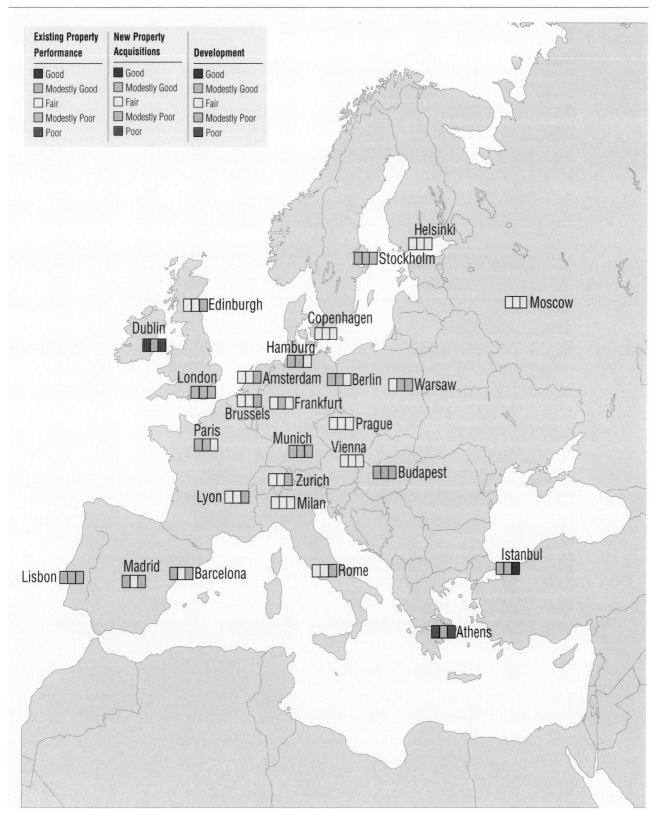

Existing Property Performance
- Good
- Modestly Good
- Fair
- Modestly Poor
- Poor

New Property Acquisitions
- Good
- Modestly Good
- Fair
- Modestly Poor
- Poor

Development
- Good
- Modestly Good
- Fair
- Modestly Poor
- Poor

EXHIBIT 3-6
Best Sectors for Acquisitions by City

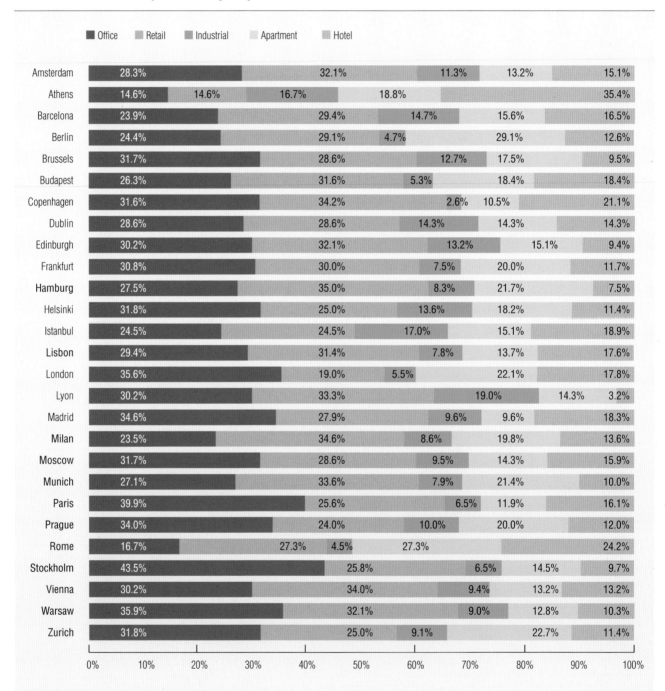

■ Office ■ Retail ■ Industrial ■ Apartment ■ Hotel

	Office	Retail	Industrial	Apartment	Hotel
Amsterdam	28.3%	32.1%	11.3%	13.2%	15.1%
Athens	14.6%	14.6%	16.7%	18.8%	35.4%
Barcelona	23.9%	29.4%	14.7%	15.6%	16.5%
Berlin	24.4%	29.1%	4.7%	29.1%	12.6%
Brussels	31.7%	28.6%	12.7%	17.5%	9.5%
Budapest	26.3%	31.6%	5.3%	18.4%	18.4%
Copenhagen	31.6%	34.2%	2.6%	10.5%	21.1%
Dublin	28.6%	28.6%	14.3%	14.3%	14.3%
Edinburgh	30.2%	32.1%	13.2%	15.1%	9.4%
Frankfurt	30.8%	30.0%	7.5%	20.0%	11.7%
Hamburg	27.5%	35.0%	8.3%	21.7%	7.5%
Helsinki	31.8%	25.0%	13.6%	18.2%	11.4%
Istanbul	24.5%	24.5%	17.0%	15.1%	18.9%
Lisbon	29.4%	31.4%	7.8%	13.7%	17.6%
London	35.6%	19.0%	5.5%	22.1%	17.8%
Lyon	30.2%	33.3%	19.0%	14.3%	3.2%
Madrid	34.6%	27.9%	9.6%	9.6%	18.3%
Milan	23.5%	34.6%	8.6%	19.8%	13.6%
Moscow	31.7%	28.6%	9.5%	14.3%	15.9%
Munich	27.1%	33.6%	7.9%	21.4%	10.0%
Paris	39.9%	25.6%	6.5%	11.9%	16.1%
Prague	34.0%	24.0%	10.0%	20.0%	12.0%
Rome	16.7%	27.3%	4.5%	27.3%	24.2%
Stockholm	43.5%	25.8%	6.5%	14.5%	9.7%
Vienna	30.2%	34.0%	9.4%	13.2%	13.2%
Warsaw	35.9%	32.1%	9.0%	12.8%	10.3%
Zurich	31.8%	25.0%	9.1%	22.7%	11.4%

0% 10% 20% 30% 40% 50% 60% 70% 80% 90% 100%

Source: *Emerging Trends in Real Estate Europe 2011* survey.

The Cities

As noted, the league tables should not be treated as having a high degree of precision. However, the survey responses do provide a guide to which markets are broadly in favour and those that are not.

Munich

Munich once again holds the top spot for performance of existing investments and also performs strongly in the other categories—third for new investment acquisitions and development. In the 2010 report, respondents commented on the strength of the German economy, but cited concerns that its fragility would become apparent as the country was weaned off state stimulus. Respondents this year seem to be taking the view that the risk has abated, and there is widespread belief that the German economy is set to perform well, driven by manufacturing exports to emerging markets. Within Germany, Munich is again preferred for its perceived stability. As one local interviewee said, "Germany will be a boring market as ever, but boring is not meant in a negative way. It will simply be stable." Despite the reservations expressed regarding the league tables, it is worth noting that survey respondents who ranked Munich generally also ranked other German cities, so there is a pretty consistent view that investors prefer it over other German cities for 2011. It is also worth noting that its perceived relative stability is not an attractive feature for everyone: Those who actively seek more volatile markets prefer Frankfurt as their top German city.

Istanbul

Istanbul ranks second for existing investments and first for both new acquisitions and development. In 2009, Istanbul had ranked high in the tables, based on the view that it would be less affected by the economic problems besetting the rest of Europe. "Economic troubles haven't had the same impact on Istanbul's commercial real estate as they have with other European locations," one interviewee commented then. By last year, that optimism had faded somewhat, and Istanbul had slipped to seventh for existing investments and fifth for new acquisitions. Its recovery to such a high ranking in the tables this year may appear counterintuitive in view of the general comments from interviewees that investors remain risk averse. Partly this can be explained by the fact that local respondents always rank Istanbul high; in a survey where fewer respondents are ranking each city, this has a greater impact. However, both local and international investors have become more positive about Istanbul since last year. It is also worth noting that interest in Istanbul as a destination for investing in industrial property has risen. For those investors who selected industrial as the preferred investment for any city, the largest number chose Istanbul. Its strong performance can also be explained by investors' reasons for optimism about investments in the city. As noted, the general sentiment for most of Europe is that investment success will be achieved despite stagnant underlying fundamentals through careful stock selection and asset management. In the case of Turkey, those investors who remain fans

EXHIBIT 3-7
Munich

	Prospects	Rating	Ranking
Existing Property Performance	Modestly Good	6.08	1st
New Property Acquisitions	Modestly Good	5.97	3rd
Development Prospects	Modestly Good	5.73	3rd

Best Sector for Acquisitions in 2011

Retail **33.6%**   Apartment Residential (Rental) **21.4%**

Office **27.1%**   Industrial/Distribution **7.9%**   Hotels **10%**

Investment Prospects

Source: *Emerging Trends in Real Estate Europe 2011* survey.

EXHIBIT 3-8
Istanbul

	Prospects	Rating	Ranking
Existing Property Performance	Modestly Good	6.08	2nd
New Property Acquisitions	Modestly Good	6.38	1st
Development Prospects	Good	6.63	1st

Best Sector for Acquisitions in 2011

Retail **24.5%**   Apartment Residential (Rental) **15.1%**

Office **24.5%**   Industrial/Distribution **17.0%**   Hotels **18.9%**

Investment Prospects

Source: *Emerging Trends in Real Estate Europe 2011* survey.

do so because of the underlying fundamentals. It is one of the few markets where investors remain confident in the city rather than in their own ability to buck the general trend through superior real estate investment skills.

London

London places third for existing property performance, and second for new property acquisitions and development. Last year, sentiment for London had improved dramatically, and indeed many respondents were worried that the market was overheating, certainly for prime properties. This year, many respondents continue to favour London, particularly for prime. As one interviewee observed, "London is a country in itself and seems to defy gravity." Others remain concerned that London is overpriced, but are also concerned by the economic fundamentals outside the South East. As one interviewee commented, "I think the austerity measures are disproportionately going to affect the regions. So London versus the rest of U.K. will be more extreme than we have ever seen it." For some investors, this represents an opportunity. "The U.K. market has been driven up by capital pouring into retail funds," one observed. "This has generally gone for prime assets in London. These do not present much attraction for an opportunistic investor. Regionally, there is more to go for if you can buy good stock to which you can bring good asset management skills." Another com-

mented, "Clearly, regional office markets or anywhere outside South East will be harder hit. But if that is in the price, potentially that is interesting for us."

Last year, the report noted that whilst sentiment for development was generally falling across Europe, London was an exception. The report last year noted that the return of confidence in London had been sufficient for investors to again consider development, with one saying, "Somebody is going to shoot me, but now is the time to do some development in the City: not much good stock available once existing is absorbed." Said another, "We have high expectations that we will start development next year." A number of developments did start or restart in London in 2010, and sentiment remains positive for 2011.

The breadth of response regarding London is extensive. It received the largest number of survey responses in each of the categories, with responses from both local and international investors.

Paris

Last year, the report commented that Paris was "seen as having a broader economic base than London and is less dependent on the financial services sector. As one investor commented, 'It is seen as being less volatile than the U.K., and there are still good opportunities there despite there being limited stock on the market. This is likely to continue into 2010. This market is displaying similar characteristics

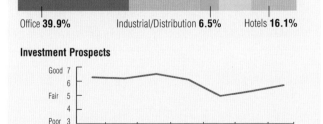

EXHIBIT 3-9
London

	Prospects	Rating	Ranking
Existing Property Performance	Modestly Good	5.87	3rd
New Property Acquisitions	Modestly Good	6.08	2nd
Development Prospects	Modestly Good	5.74	2nd

Best Sector for Acquisitions in 2011

Retail **19.0%**   Apartment Residential (Rental) **22.1%**

Office **35.6%**   Industrial/Distribution **5.5%**   Hotels **17.8%**

Investment Prospects

Good 7
6
Fair 5
4
Poor 3
2005 2006 2007 2008 2009 2010 2011

Source: *Emerging Trends in Real Estate Europe 2011* survey.

EXHIBIT 3-10
Paris

	Prospects	Rating	Ranking
Existing Property Performance	Modestly Good	5.79	4th
New Property Acquisitions	Modestly Good	5.67	8th
Development Prospects	Fair	5.42	7th

Best Sector for Acquisitions in 2011

Retail **25.6%**   Apartment Residential (Rental) **11.9%**

Office **39.9%**   Industrial/Distribution **6.5%**   Hotels **16.1%**

Investment Prospects

Good 7
6
Fair 5
4
Poor 3
2005 2006 2007 2008 2009 2010 2011

Source: *Emerging Trends in Real Estate Europe 2011* survey.

to London at the present time.'" This indeed was much how 2010 played out, with core money heading for Paris, particularly at the point when London was seen as most overpriced. Core money is expected to continue to flow into Paris, a city that, as one interviewee said, displays "less volatility, less risk, therefore more stability, but it means less profit." For the same reason, more opportunistic investors seeking higher returns generally see it as being as unattractive as London.

Stockholm

Many respondents have positive attitudes toward the Nordic economies, which are believed to have weathered the economic storm better than other parts of Europe. "In terms of economies, we like the Nordic region— Scandinavia plus Finland—the best," one interviewee said. "Those countries have less debt to begin with. Those countries are also managed better, they invest in more industries, they spend more on research and education, so we are very positive on the Nordic region overall." Within the region, Stockholm is seen as having the deepest market. A theme that runs through interviews from local players in Stockholm is that they believe that 2010 was a lot better than expected, but that 2011 will be worse. However, it should be noted that pessimism followed by pleasant surprise was a feature of Nordic interviewees last year, too.

Hamburg, Berlin, and Frankfurt

As noted, there is broad positive sentiment regarding the strength of the German economy, with Munich ranked first for existing property performance. Hamburg, Berlin, and Frankfurt are clustered together at sixth, seventh,

EXHIBIT 3-12
Hamburg

	Prospects	Rating	Ranking
Existing Property Performance	Modestly Good	5.69	6th
New Property Acquisitions	Modestly Good	5.70	7th
Development Prospects	Fair	5.30	8th

Best Sector for Acquisitions in 2011

Retail **35.0%**   Apartment Residential (Rental) **21.7%**

Office **27.5%**   Industrial/Distribution **8.3%**   Hotels **7.5%**

Investment Prospects

Source: *Emerging Trends in Real Estate Europe 2011* survey.

EXHIBIT 3-11
Stockholm

	Prospects	Rating	Ranking
Existing Property Performance	Modestly Good	5.73	5th
New Property Acquisitions	Modestly Good	5.96	4th
Development Prospects	Modestly Good	5.53	6th

Best Sector for Acquisitions in 2011

Retail **25.8%**   Apartment Residential (Rental) **14.5%**

Office **43.5%**   Industrial/Distribution **6.5%**   Hotels **9.7%**

Investment Prospects

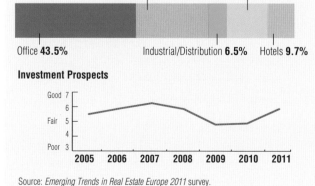

Source: *Emerging Trends in Real Estate Europe 2011* survey.

EXHIBIT 3-13
Berlin

	Prospects	Rating	Ranking
Existing Property Performance	Modestly Good	5.58	7th
New Property Acquisitions	Modestly Good	5.72	5th
Development Prospects	Fair	5.13	10th

Best Sector for Acquisitions in 2011

Retail **29.1%**   Apartment Residential (Rental) **29.1%**

Office **24.4%**   Industrial/Distribution **4.7%**   Hotels **12.6%**

Investment Prospects

Source: *Emerging Trends in Real Estate Europe 2011* survey.

EXHIBIT 3-14
Frankfurt

	Prospects	Rating	Ranking
Existing Property Performance	Fair	5.36	8th (tie)
New Property Acquisitions	Modestly Good	5.55	9th
Development Prospects	Fair	4.88	13th

Best Sector for Acquisitions in 2011

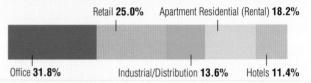

Retail **30.0%** Apartment Residential (Rental) **20.0%**

Office **30.8%** Industrial/Distribution **7.5%** Hotels **11.7%**

Investment Prospects

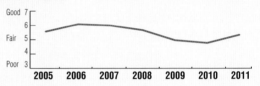

Source: *Emerging Trends in Real Estate Europe 2011* survey.

EXHIBIT 3-15
Helsinki

	Prospects	Rating	Ranking
Existing Property Performance	Fair	5.36	8th (tie)
New Property Acquisitions	Fair	5.33	14th
Development Prospects	Modestly Good	4.77	14th

Best Sector for Acquisitions in 2011

Retail **25.0%** Apartment Residential (Rental) **18.2%**

Office **31.8%** Industrial/Distribution **13.6%** Hotels **11.4%**

Investment Prospects

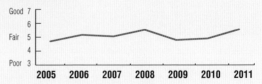

Source: *Emerging Trends in Real Estate Europe 2011* survey.

and eighth, respectively. As in 2010, Berlin is particularly favoured for residential; it is the city in the survey with the highest proportion of respondents identifying residential as the preferred asset type.

Helsinki

Helsinki benefits from the general positive sentiment among investors for the economic performance and outlook for the Nordics.

Warsaw

Central and eastern Europe remains generally somewhat out of favour, as it was in 2010. As was the case in the 2010 report, Warsaw is regarded as having better prospects than the rest of the region, particularly as the German economy improves. It has risen up the table for existing asset performance from 13th to tenth. As in 2010, Warsaw ranks fourth for development. Comments from interviewees included, "I don't see Poland's great run ending"; "Poland for me is not central eastern Europe; it is Europe. A growing economy with cheap labour, and it is not overbuilt. For me it is doing very well"; "Poland has not really had a crisis, more of a slowing down"; and "Warsaw—good or very good prospects. The demand is growing and will exceed the supply; the supply is limited due to banks which are not keen to finance developments. Effective rents will rise and will get closer to headline rents."

EXHIBIT 3-16
Warsaw

	Prospects	Rating	Ranking
Existing Property Performance	Fair	5.35	10th
New Property Acquisitions	Modestly Good	5.71	6th
Development Prospects	Modestly Good	5.58	4th

Best Sector for Acquisitions in 2011

Retail **32.1%** Apartment Residential (Rental) **12.8%**

Office **35.9%** Industrial/Distribution **9.0%** Hotels **10.3%**

Investment Prospects

Source: *Emerging Trends in Real Estate Europe 2011* survey.

There is a risk that Poland may be slightly a victim of its own recent success. "We have bought quite a bit in 2008 and 2009, and don't want to overallocate," one interviewee commented. Another expressed concern that Poland might be too much "flavour of the month": "People maybe think they can raise money if they say 'We like Poland.' We've done a deal there and are shaping it up to sell to a rush of capital coming. How many people can be building out in Poland?"

Zurich

Zurich sits in 11th spot for existing property, as it did in 2010. As is the case with a number of cities ranked from tenth to 20th in the tables, it does not excite strong views from interviewees or survey respondents. In view of the general comments regarding the nature of the survey responses, paying undue attention to the relative positioning of the mid-performing cities would, in any case, perhaps be misleading. Zurich holds the distinction of being the city that garnered the fewest ratings in the survey responses.

Moscow

In 2008, Moscow was the highest-ranked city in the survey, with respondents believing that high oil prices would drive the economy and keep the real estate market immune from the problems besetting the rest of Europe. In 2009 and 2010, that optimism had evaporated and Moscow had slipped to 24th in the table for existing property performance. However, even last year there was positive sentiment for the longer term, particularly from local investors, citing the view that recovery in commodity prices would drive economic and occupier recovery. Whilst some respondents remain gloomy about Moscow this year, others, both local and international, see the economy improving. "Russia has huge growth potential and expected growth of more than 4 percent," one interviewee observed. This is expected to give rise to opportunities. "Moscow is improving; tenant demand is getting stronger and looks likely to grow further," one interviewee commented. "On the other side, supply is restricted (no money to build), hence the rents should rise." Said another: "Moscow has rebounded quickly in 2010, and I expect that to continue in 2011. This is being led by the office market, but there is growth in industrial and retail markets, too—constrained by the amount of space available." The change in regime in Moscow is also encouraging positive sentiment. Said one interviewee, "With the arrival of the new mayor, there are many improvements expected starting from 2011. This relates both to the infrastructure and to the expected new 'rules of the game.'"

EXHIBIT 3-17
Zurich

	Prospects	Rating	Ranking
Existing Property Performance	Fair	5.31	11th
New Property Acquisitions	Fair	5.41	11th
Development Prospects	Modestly Good	5.57	5th

Best Sector for Acquisitions in 2011

Retail **25.0%**   Apartment Residential (Rental) **22.7%**

Office **31.8%**   Industrial/Distribution **9.1%**   Hotels **11.4%**

Investment Prospects

Source: *Emerging Trends in Real Estate Europe 2011* survey.

EXHIBIT 3-18
Moscow

	Prospects	Rating	Ranking
Existing Property Performance	Fair	5.18	12th
New Property Acquisitions	Fair	5.39	12th
Development Prospects	Fair	5.20	9th

Best Sector for Acquisitions in 2011

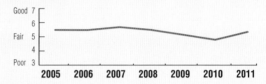

Retail **28.6%**   Apartment Residential (Rental) **14.3%**

Office **31.7%**   Industrial/Distribution **9.5%**   Hotels **15.9%**

Investment Prospects

Source: *Emerging Trends in Real Estate Europe 2011* survey.

Vienna

Like Zurich, Vienna attracted a relatively low number of survey responses and does not excite strong views from respondents. As one respondent commented, "Vienna will stay as boring (stable) as usual." A number of interviewees—particularly German investors—see the Austrian market as being particularly tied to the German one and therefore benefiting from the strengthening German economy.

Copenhagen

Like Helsinki, Copenhagen benefits from the general positive sentiment among many investors for the economic performance and outlook for the Nordics, but is also another city that does not excite strong opinions either way. "Copenhagen is expected to recover slowly—primarily for residential—whereas office buildings are still facing tough times," said one interviewee.

Lyon

Over the years, Lyon has displayed a high degree of volatility in terms of respondents' sentiment as secondary cities have moved in and out of favour.

EXHIBIT 3-20
Copenhagen

	Prospects	Rating	Ranking
Existing Property Performance	Fair	5.12	14th
New Property Acquisitions	Fair	5.45	10th
Development Prospects	Fair	4.70	15th

Best Sector for Acquisitions in 2011

Retail **34.2%** Apartment Residential (Rental) **10.5%**

Office **31.6%** Industrial/Distribution **2.6%** Hotels **21.1%**

Investment Prospects

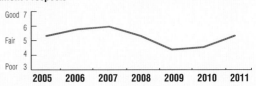

Source: *Emerging Trends in Real Estate Europe 2011* survey.

EXHIBIT 3-19
Vienna

	Prospects	Rating	Ranking
Existing Property Performance	Fair	5.15	13th
New Property Acquisitions	Fair	5.31	15th
Development Prospects	Fair	4.92	12th

Best Sector for Acquisitions in 2011

Retail **34.0%** Apartment Residential (Rental) **13.2%**

Office **30.2%** Industrial/Distribution **9.4%** Hotels **13.2%**

Investment Prospects

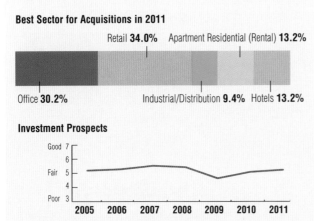

Source: *Emerging Trends in Real Estate Europe 2011* survey.

EXHIBIT 3-21
Lyon

	Prospects	Rating	Ranking
Existing Property Performance	Fair	5.04	15th
New Property Acquisitions	Fair	5.02	17th
Development Prospects	Modestly Poor	4.46	18th

Best Sector for Acquisitions in 2011

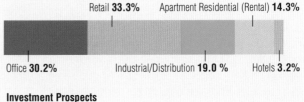

Retail **33.3%** Apartment Residential (Rental) **14.3%**

Office **30.2%** Industrial/Distribution **19.0 %** Hotels **3.2%**

Investment Prospects

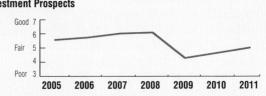

Source: *Emerging Trends in Real Estate Europe 2011* survey.

EXHIBIT 3-22
Milan

	Prospects	Rating	Ranking
Existing Property Performance	Fair	4.98	16th
New Property Acquisitions	Fair	5.04	16th
Development Prospects	Fair	4.51	16th

Best Sector for Acquisitions in 2011

Retail **34.6%**   Apartment Residential (Rental) **19.8%**

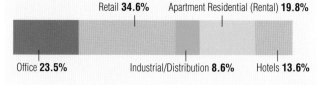

Office **23.5%**   Industrial/Distribution **8.6%**   Hotels **13.6%**

Investment Prospects

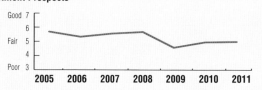

Source: *Emerging Trends in Real Estate Europe 2011* survey.

EXHIBIT 3-23
Prague

	Prospects	Rating	Ranking
Existing Property Performance	Fair	4.92	17th
New Property Acquisitions	Fair	5.38	13th
Development Prospects	Fair	5.04	11th

Best Sector for Acquisitions in 2011

Retail **24.0%**   Apartment Residential (Rental) **20.0%**

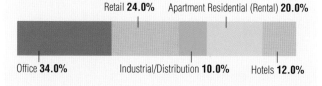

Office **34.0%**   Industrial/Distribution **10.0%**   Hotels **12.0%**

Investment Prospects

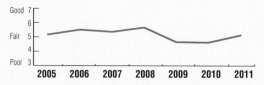

Source: *Emerging Trends in Real Estate Europe 2011* survey.

Milan

Views differ regarding Milan—and, indeed, Italy more generally. Some respondents see the country as being part of the troubled southern or peripheral European countries and therefore off the radar for investment. Many others see Italy as being in a stronger position than Spain and Portugal, although even for these people there is a question as to when to invest. "Italy economically will stay in slow lane for immediate term," said one interviewee. Another sees potential benefits for Milan from the impending Expo 2015. As with other cities, there is clearly a distinction between prime and secondary assets. "The investment market remains polarised, with demand for well-located, prime product holding firm, whereas demand for secondary stock is extremely weak," one interviewee noted.

Prague

Although not receiving the same positive attention as Warsaw, Prague is also recognised by a number of respondents as having better prospects than the rest of central and eastern Europe. Like Poland, the Czech Republic is seen as a beneficiary of the German recovery. One Czech interviewee described Germany as "one of the motors of Europe, the engine house." However, several respondents sounded a note of caution, suggesting that the Czech Republic's financial recovery could be more fragile than that of Poland. "The Czech economy may not be as immune to the financial crisis as it thinks," one interviewee said. "If one of the big automotive players or finance houses were to relocate somewhere else—like to Poland, for example—that could be a really big issue."

Rome

The comments for Milan on the general state of the Italian economy apply equally to Rome. As in previous years, respondents comment on the importance to the Rome market of the government as a tenant. It is also suggested that there are opportunities in the residential sector.

Edinburgh

For the majority of investors, secondary cities remain out of favour. This includes Edinburgh.

Brussels

As noted in the 2010 report, Brussels consistently ranks as average. Over the years, it has hovered around the middle of the rankings—sometimes toward the upper end of average, sometimes toward the lower end. This year it is toward the lower end.

EXHIBIT 3-24
Rome

	Prospects	Rating	Ranking
Existing Property Performance	Fair	4.81	18th
New Property Acquisitions	Fair	4.98	19th (tie)
Development Prospects	Modestly Poor	4.47	17th

Best Sector for Acquisitions in 2011

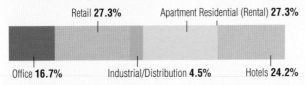

Retail **27.3%** Apartment Residential (Rental) **27.3%**

Office **16.7%** Industrial/Distribution **4.5%** Hotels **24.2%**

Investment Prospects

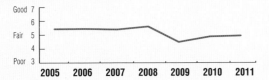

Source: *Emerging Trends in Real Estate Europe 2011* survey.

EXHIBIT 3-26
Brussels

	Prospects	Rating	Ranking
Existing Property Performance	Fair	4.69	20th
New Property Acquisitions	Fair	4.92	22nd
Development Prospects	Modestly Poor	4.18	20th

Best Sector for Acquisitions in 2011

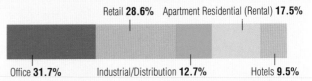

Retail **28.6%** Apartment Residential (Rental) **17.5%**

Office **31.7%** Industrial/Distribution **12.7%** Hotels **9.5%**

Investment Prospects

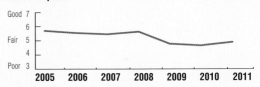

Source: *Emerging Trends in Real Estate Europe 2011* survey.

EXHIBIT 3-25
Edinburgh

	Prospects	Rating	Ranking
Existing Property Performance	Fair	4.72	19th
New Property Acquisitions	Fair	4.71	23rd
Development Prospects	Modestly Poor	3.73	22nd

Best Sector for Acquisitions in 2011

Retail **32.1%** Apartment Residential (Rental) **15.1%**

Office **30.2%** Industrial/Distribution **13.2%** Hotels **9.4%**

Investment Prospects

Source: *Emerging Trends in Real Estate Europe 2011* survey.

EXHIBIT 3-27
Amsterdam

	Prospects	Rating	Ranking
Existing Property Performance	Fair	4.65	21st
New Property Acquisitions	Fair	4.98	19th (tie)
Development Prospects	Modestly Poor	4.27	19th

Best Sector for Acquisitions in 2011

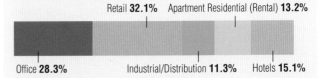

Retail **32.1%** Apartment Residential (Rental) **13.2%**

Office **28.3%** Industrial/Distribution **11.3%** Hotels **15.1%**

Investment Prospects

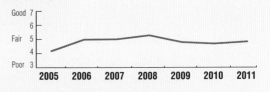

Source: *Emerging Trends in Real Estate Europe 2011* survey.

EXHIBIT 3-28
Madrid

	Prospects	Rating	Ranking
Existing Property Performance	Modestly Poor	4.32	22nd
New Property Acquisitions	Fair	5.00	18th
Development Prospects	Modestly Poor	3.58	25th

Best Sector for Acquisitions in 2011

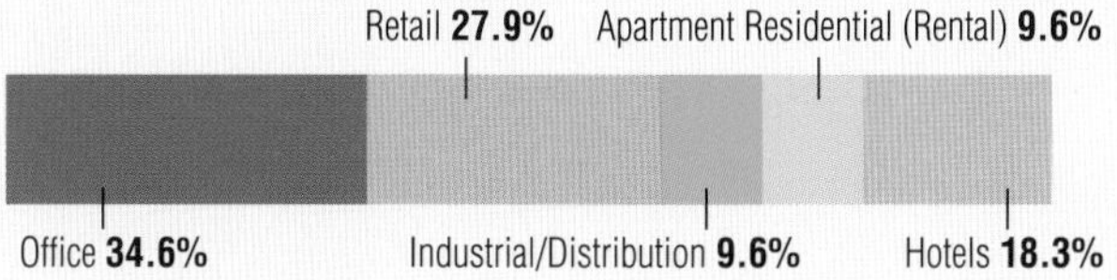
Retail 27.9%
Apartment Residential (Rental) 9.6%
Office 34.6%
Industrial/Distribution 9.6%
Hotels 18.3%

Investment Prospects

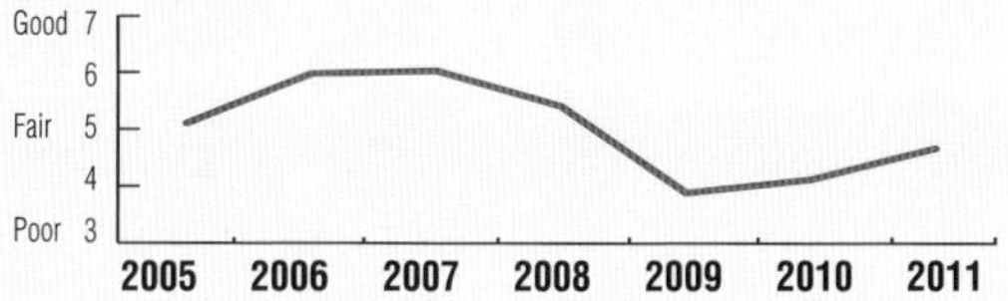
Good 7
6
Fair 5
4
Poor 3
2005 2006 2007 2008 2009 2010 2011

Source: *Emerging Trends in Real Estate Europe 2011* survey.

EXHIBIT 3-29
Barcelona

	Prospects	Rating	Ranking
Existing Property Performance	Modestly Poor	4.21	23rd
New Property Acquisitions	Fair	4.93	21st
Development Prospects	Modestly Poor	3.58	24th

Best Sector for Acquisitions in 2011

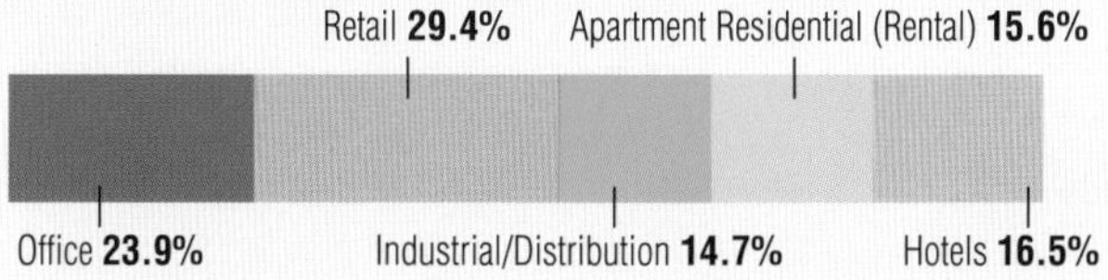
Retail 29.4%
Apartment Residential (Rental) 15.6%
Office 23.9%
Industrial/Distribution 14.7%
Hotels 16.5%

Investment Prospects

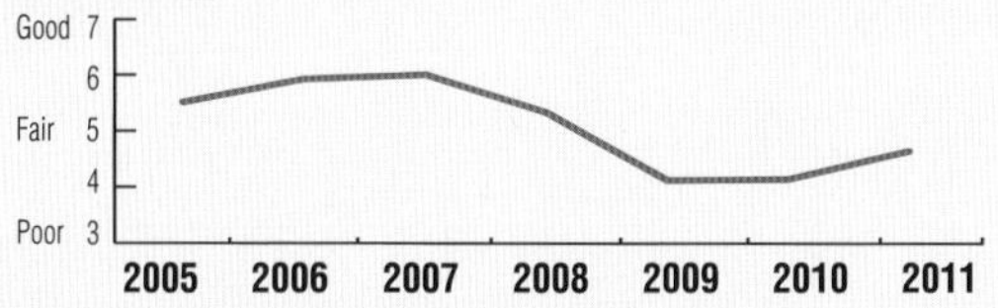
Good 7
6
Fair 5
4
Poor 3
2005 2006 2007 2008 2009 2010 2011

Source: *Emerging Trends in Real Estate Europe 2011* survey.

Amsterdam

Like Brussels, Amsterdam is usually among the middle-ranking cities. Local respondents are keen to emphasise that Amsterdam should be seen as a proxy for the broader Randstad conurbation—Amsterdam, the Hague, Rotterdam, and Utrecht.

Madrid and Barcelona

Some interviewees see signs of hope for the Spanish economy, one commenting that things are "definitely past the worst in Spain." However, the more general view is that Spain is one of the "peripheral countries" that is struggling. Local respondents are also pessimistic about Spain's short-term prospects. A number of interviewees comment on the overreliance on the construction industry as a driver of the economy in the boom years. "Spain and Portugal will have to move their economies out of construction into other segments, which is a long-term process," said one. Added another, "For Spain, there is no natural replacement for construction as part of economic growth, but tourism is a big feature. Its connections with Latin America should not be forgotten; that is a big growth area for corporations. Spain has always had high unemployment."

The broad sentiment can be summed up by one major, international fund manager: "Spain is the place we have the biggest concerns and the most negative views. Our view is there is low likelihood we will be positively surprised; a high likelihood could be more negative. [On] GDP growth assumptions, the consensus forecast is it recovers in 2012, but I wouldn't be surprised if it gets pushed out further. Therefore, investing in new developments in Spain is something we wouldn't do. One area is distressed acquisitions, if there are any, and so far there have not been many. Whatever made up the growth over the past years isn't there anymore. The construction industry is heavily impacted, there is no doubt about it; personal households are indebted, and the mess hasn't surfaced with the banks."

On a more positive note, some more opportunistic investors are starting to see the possibilities of investments emerging and are looking for deals from the Spanish banks.

EXHIBIT 3-30
Lisbon

	Prospects	Rating	Ranking
Existing Property Performance	Modestly Poor	4.04	24th
New Property Acquisitions	Modestly Poor	4.30	25th
Development Prospects	Modestly Poor	3.64	23rd

Best Sector for Acquisitions in 2011

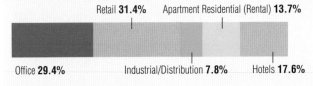

Retail **31.4%**　　Apartment Residential (Rental) **13.7%**

Office **29.4%**　　Industrial/Distribution **7.8%**　　Hotels **17.6%**

Investment Prospects

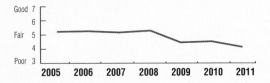

Source: *Emerging Trends in Real Estate Europe 2011* survey.

Lisbon
Respondents and interviewees have little positive to say about the economy or the local market prospects. It does not seem to be on the radar for opportunistic investors in the way that Spain is for some.

Budapest
As noted, central and eastern Europe remains broadly out of favour. As was the case in 2009 and 2010, Budapest is not seen as having the positive features that help differentiate Warsaw, Moscow, or even Prague.

Athens
Although Athens ranked 20th out of 27 cities in the 2010 report, many respondents expressed concerns about the fragility of the Greek economy and fears that matters could take a significant turn for the worse. Those worries proved well-founded. Local respondents are universally gloomy, almost all suggesting that 2011 will be worse than 2010.

EXHIBIT 3-31
Budapest

	Prospects	Rating	Ranking
Existing Property Performance	Modestly Poor	3.89	25th
New Property Acquisitions	Modestly Poor	4.35	24th
Development Prospects	Modestly Poor	3.74	21st

Best Sector for Acquisitions in 2011

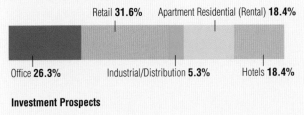

Retail **31.6%**　　Apartment Residential (Rental) **18.4%**

Office **26.3%**　　Industrial/Distribution **5.3%**　　Hotels **18.4%**

Investment Prospects

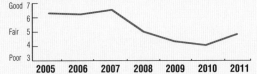

Source: *Emerging Trends in Real Estate Europe 2011* survey.

EXHIBIT 3-32
Athens

	Prospects	Rating	Ranking
Existing Property Performance	Poor	3.32	26th
New Property Acquisitions	Modestly Poor	3.84	26th
Development Prospects	Poor	2.97	26th

Best Sector for Acquisitions in 2011

Retail **14.6%**　　Apartment Residential (Rental) **18.8%**

Office **14.6%**　　Industrial/Distribution **16.7%**　　Hotels **35.4%**

Investment Prospects

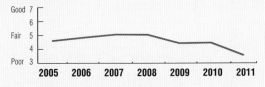

Source: *Emerging Trends in Real Estate Europe 2011* survey.

EXHIBIT 3-33
Dublin

	Prospects	Rating	Ranking
Existing Property Performance	Poor	2.85	27th
New Property Acquisitions	Modestly Poor	3.63	27th
Development Prospects	Very Poor	2.45	27th

Best Sector for Acquisitions in 2011

Retail **28.6%**   Apartment Residential (Rental) **14.3%**

Office **28.6%**   Industrial/Distribution **14.3%**   Hotels **14.3%**

Investment Prospects

Source: *Emerging Trends in Real Estate Europe 2011* survey.

Dublin

In 2009, Dublin was rated lowest of the 27 cities evaluated, for both investment and development, with one investor saying, "Ireland's a real struggle, a bubble that's popped." Despite a slight improvement in sentiment in the 2010 report for investment, the city remained in 27th spot for the performance of existing assets. Last year prospects for new acquisitions were slightly better, with some overseas investors positive about the opportunities. "Ireland has strengths that people are not seeing and end up focussing on its major downsides," said one interviewee. Unfortunately, the major downsides have become more evident over the year, and Dublin has slipped back to 27th place for all the categories.

Property Types in Perspective

"Investors wanting to buy are looking for core, perhaps even core-plus."

"Other than residential for defensive qualities, there isn't a sector play. It is individual deals and timing," said one interviewee. And these deals are most likely to occur in the core and core-plus segment. Regarding the relative prospects for the different strategic options, votes for core and core-plus outnumber their riskier counterparts—value-add and opportunistic—by about 3 to 1. Among the comments from those interviewed: "Demand for core is as hot as ever"; "There is movement in the market, but only for core properties"; "Core with focus on quality"; "Investors wanting to buy are looking for core, perhaps even core-plus"; "Core and core-plus are hot"; "All money is going into safe-haven structures"; "In general, lower-risk strategies will be favoured"; and "Institutional investors are very risk averse—only fully let properties in prime locations."

These sentiments are likely to carry into 2011. "Core investments will remain king," one interviewee said. Said another, "There is still a lot of work to do in core; there are still many markets which have not been explored."

Sector Outlook

How is this being translated into property sectors? In the interviews, core was frequently cited to mean city offices, street retail, and shopping centres. The other categories drew considerably fewer comments. In the quantitative analysis of the survey, all major property types were credited with improved investment prospects. In terms of performance prospects, the spread between the property types has narrowed: all sectors are seen to offer "fair" value. Retail takes the pole position, followed closely by offices. Rental apartments, last year's top category, dropped to

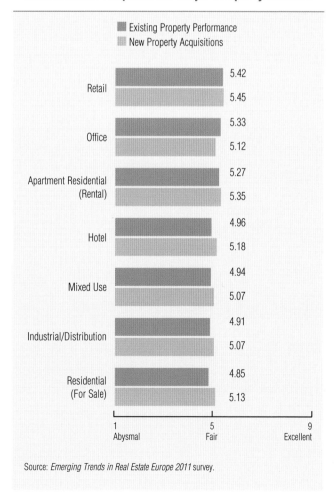

EXHIBIT 4-1
Investment Prospects for Major Property Sectors

- Existing Property Performance
- New Property Acquisitions

Retail	Existing	5.42
	New	5.45
Office	Existing	5.33
	New	5.12
Apartment Residential (Rental)	Existing	5.27
	New	5.35
Hotel	Existing	4.96
	New	5.18
Mixed Use	Existing	4.94
	New	5.07
Industrial/Distribution	Existing	4.91
	New	5.07
Residential (For Sale)	Existing	4.85
	New	5.13

1 Abysmal   5 Fair   9 Excellent

Source: *Emerging Trends in Real Estate Europe 2011* survey.

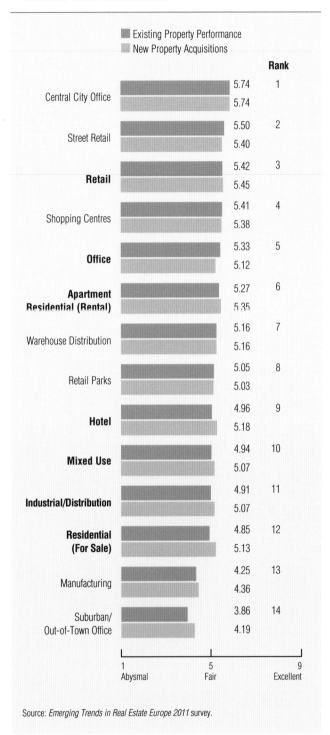

EXHIBIT 4-2

Investment Prospects for Major Property Sectors and Subsectors

■ Existing Property Performance
■ New Property Acquisitions

	Existing	New	Rank
Central City Office	5.74	5.74	1
Street Retail	5.50	5.40	2
Retail	5.42	5.45	3
Shopping Centres	5.41	5.38	4
Office	5.33	5.12	5
Apartment Residential (Rental)	5.27	5.35	6
Warehouse Distribution	5.16	5.16	7
Retail Parks	5.05	5.03	8
Hotel	4.96	5.18	9
Mixed Use	4.94	5.07	10
Industrial/Distribution	4.91	5.07	11
Residential (For Sale)	4.85	5.13	12
Manufacturing	4.25	4.36	13
Suburban/ Out-of-Town Office	3.86	4.19	14

1	5	9
Abysmal	Fair	Excellent

Source: *Emerging Trends in Real Estate Europe 2011* survey.

third place. There is a noticeable gap between the medallists and the also-ran sectors—hotels, mixed use, industrial/distribution, and for-sale residential. (See exhibit 4-1.)

New acquisitions are seen to hold slightly better prospects than existing property holdings, central-city offices being the one exception. Among the subsectors, the performance outlook on new acquisitions for city offices is rated "modestly good," followed in order by street retail and shopping centres, indicating that core locations are likely to remain the flavour of the month. Hotels and warehouse distribution facilities are the highest climbers, moving four places each into the middle ranks. This may reflect an improved economic outlook for some of the main European markets. Retail parks, often in out-of-town locations, dropped to 12th place. While they are still considered to offer "fair" prospects, the other peripheral assets such as manufacturing and suburban/out-of-town offices are rated to achieve no more than a "modestly poor" performance. "It probably accentuates the gap between the good and the bad; because the bad is becoming [worse], the gap is widening," one interviewee said.

Development

Creating core quality by development "is compelling, if opportunities arise in prime locations," but "development will continue to have problems as banks are reluctant to finance new projects due to economic uncertainty and

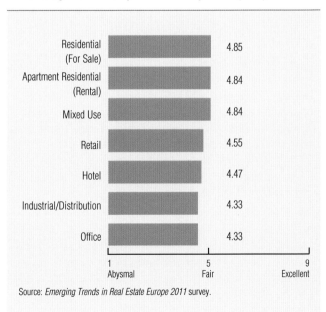

EXHIBIT 4-3

Development Prospects for Major Property Sectors

Residential (For Sale)	4.85
Apartment Residential (Rental)	4.84
Mixed Use	4.84
Retail	4.55
Hotel	4.47
Industrial/Distribution	4.33
Office	4.33

1	5	9
Abysmal	Fair	Excellent

Source: *Emerging Trends in Real Estate Europe 2011* survey.

remaining risks on banks' balance sheets." All sectors show improved ratings on their development potential, with the top eight being identified as holding "fair" prospects. Central offices take the lead, followed by for-sale residential properties and rental apartments. The outlook for manufacturing is "modestly poor," while suburban/out-of-town offices, with no more than a "poor" rating, are no longer classified as a development option at all.

Cap Rates

On average, cap rates are now around 70 basis points below those forecast last year. Driven by strong demand, "the very top end of the market pricing is as aggressive as it has ever been." "Yields came down much faster than we anticipated." For 2011, survey participants expect yields to remain largely at the current level, with cap rate movements mostly in the single-digit range. The biggest impediment "is finding the right assets at reasonable prices"—a stance frequently cited. Among the comments:

EXHIBIT 4-4
Development Prospects for Major Property Sectors and Subsectors

Source: *Emerging Trends in Real Estate Europe 2011* survey.

EXHIBIT 4-5
Prospects for Prime Yields

	Cap Rate/ Prime Yields Nov. 2010 (Percentage)	Expected Cap Rate/ Prime Yields Dec. 2011 (Percentage)	Expected Cap Rate/ Prime Yield Shift (Basis Points)
Apartment Residential (Rental)	5.26	5.36	10
Office	6.65	6.55	-9
Central City Office	6.30	6.14	-16
Suburban/Out-of-Town Office	7.54	7.54	-1
Retail	6.80	6.72	-8
Shopping Centres	6.70	6.60	-10
Retail Parks	7.24	7.22	-3
Street Retail	6.43	6.41	-2
Hotel	7.01	7.15	13
Mixed Use	7.33	7.37	5
Industrial/Distribution	8.02	7.93	-9
Warehouse Distribution	7.88	7.79	-9
Manufacturing	8.32	8.26	-6

Source: *Emerging Trends in Real Estate Europe 2011* survey.

the "challenge is to ensure access to core properties—that you are shown properties before they come to the market"; "Everybody wants core; to find good deals in the segment is difficult"; "Core will be overpriced due to too much demand from conservative investors"; and "We also have to invest in core; you can't get anything else approved at the moment. It is always the question whether you are buying too expensively."

Going Green

Sustainability features have moved higher on the agenda of investors and developers. However, sustainability is more linked to new development and new acquisitions. "If it is brand new asset, there is no way that we are going to buy something that is not green. But this represents only 2 percent of the market," one interviewee said. "Green is the new standard. Anything that doesn't meet green criteria is

EXHIBIT 4-6
Best Acquisition Opportunities by Sector and City in 2011

	Office	Retail	Industrial	Apartment	Hotel	Highest Percentage for Any Sector in the City	Best Sector for Acquisition in the City
Paris	**10.5%**	**7.1%**	**5.6%**	**5.3%**	**8.9%**	10.5%	Office
Berlin	4.9%	**6.1%**	3.0%	**9.8%**	**5.2%**	9.8%	Apartment
London	**9.1%**	**5.1%**	4.5%	**9.5%**	**9.5%**	9.5%	Apartment
Istanbul	4.1%	4.3%	**9.1%**	4.2%	**6.6%**	9.1%	Industrial
Barcelona	4.1%	**5.3%**	**8.1%**	4.5%	**5.9%**	8.1%	Industrial
Munich	**6.0%**	**7.7%**	**5.6%**	**7.9%**	4.6%	7.9%	Apartment
Hamburg	**5.2%**	**6.9%**	**5.1%**	**6.9%**	3.0%	6.9%	Retail
Frankfurt	**5.8%**	**5.9%**	4.5%	**6.3%**	4.6%	6.3%	Apartment
Madrid	**5.6%**	4.8%	**5.1%**	2.6%	**6.2%**	6.2%	Hotel
Lyon	3.0%	3.5%	**6.1%**	2.4%	0.7%	6.1%	Industrial
Athens	1.1%	1.2%	4.0%	2.4%	**5.6%**	5.6%	Hotel
Rome	1.7%	3.0%	1.5%	4.8%	**5.2%**	5.2%	Hotel
Milan	3.0%	4.6%	3.5%	4.2%	3.6%	4.6%	Retail
Warsaw	4.4%	4.1%	3.5%	2.6%	2.6%	4.4%	Office
Stockholm	4.2%	2.6%	2.0%	2.4%	2.0%	4.2%	Office
Brussels	3.1%	3.0%	4.0%	2.9%	2.0%	4.0%	Industrial
Edinburgh	2.5%	2.8%	3.5%	2.1%	1.6%	3.5%	Industrial
Moscow	3.1%	3.0%	3.0%	2.4%	3.3%	3.3%	Hotel
Helsinki	2.2%	1.8%	3.0%	2.1%	1.6%	3.0%	Industrial
Amsterdam	2.4%	2.8%	3.0%	1.9%	2.6%	3.0%	Industrial
Vienna	2.5%	3.0%	2.5%	1.9%	2.3%	3.0%	Retail
Lisbon	2.4%	2.6%	2.0%	1.9%	3.0%	3.0%	Hotel
Prague	2.7%	2.0%	2.5%	2.6%	2.0%	2.7%	Office
Zurich	2.2%	1.8%	2.0%	2.6%	1.6%	2.6%	Apartment
Copenhagen	1.9%	2.1%	0.5%	1.1%	2.6%	2.6%	Hotel
Budapest	1.6%	2.0%	1.0%	1.9%	2.3%	2.3%	Hotel
Dublin	0.9%	1.0%	1.5%	0.8%	1.0%	1.5%	Industrial
	100%	100%	100%	100%	100%		

Source: *Emerging Trends in Real Estate Europe 2011* survey.

Notes: Survey respondents were asked to choose—for any city in which they were active—one property sector that offers the best acquisition opportunities in 2011.

Any result of 5 percent or more appears in bold for easy reference.

at least second choice, if not third." "Anything that is not green will suffer in the future—perhaps not at the moment, but in time to come." But "there is still a great deal of uncertainty what criteria to use." The lack of a common standard and new technology as a moving target calls for some difficult choices. "There is [. . .] a danger that in five years' time one might choose another technology at a tenth of the price. There could be a relatively high

potential penalty for early adopters." While new buildings are easily kitted out to meet modern standards, "the crucial issue is the existing stock." So far this has not really been tackled. "I think the market is lacking know-how to address sustainability issues in existing properties. These are our problem."

EXHIBIT 4-7
European Direct Real Estate Investment by Property Type

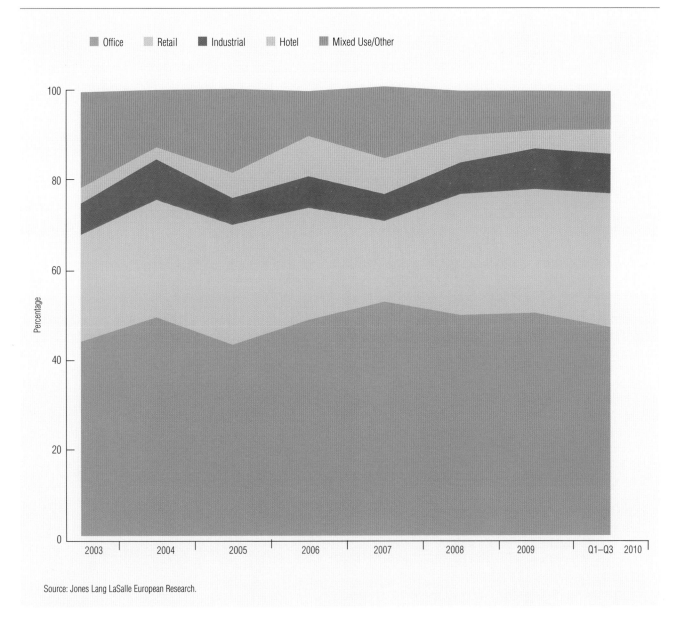

Source: Jones Lang LaSalle European Research.

Retail

"The market is playing retail," one interviewee said. Among other comments: "Retail is very, very popular at the moment because it stood up well during the crisis"; "Good-quality retail assets form backbone of portfolio"; and "Though it is a low-growth environment, rents have held up. There is good demand and the market is always evolving." Among the main property sectors, retail came out on top. But the approval is by no means unanimous, as some other comments suggest: "The market believes retail will be booming business in Europe. I am very sceptical about that"; "Retail has been surprisingly good, but the retailers can't defy gravity forever"; and "I'm worried about retail."

In the short term, there is concern about consumer spending. "Consumer spending in Europe will have [to fall] because the fiscal austerity measures mean that people's net income will be lower." "Everybody is too optimistic about retail. Up to now it was like a safe haven, but the consumer has to cut back as well, so retail will be less favoured. In my opinion, it is overpriced at the moment." "Quite pessimistic about retail. If the consumer spending is falling, something will happen to retail."

Furthermore, uncertainties about structural change in retail trade weigh on people's minds. "New technologies, the internet, demographic changes, and consumer behaviour will change the retail real estate industry rapidly and dramatically." "More and more is sold through the internet." "Also, you need to take into consideration the negative demographics in a number of countries, including Germany and eastern Europe, so there will simply be less money to be spend in future."

Street Retail

Though the sector is generally attractive, there are "different prospects for different retail segments," one interviewee observed. Street retail is the segment promising the best perspectives. It may also benefit from the trend towards increasing urbanisation. "There will always be long-term performance for good high street." "High street retailers, the big brands always look for big places in the best areas of the city, as they can pay posh rents." "High street shops are still very interesting." "Street retail is really interesting, although very fragmented. It takes an active property management." Investments in "very good high street retail in well-established and large locations will last; this holds true for the major markets in Europe."

The increase in internet shopping may open up new opportunities for convenience stores for day-to-day shopping, "such as food and nonfood items not ordered over the web." In Italy, food retail chains are moving into "medium-size city supermarkets instead of the large mall too far from the day-by-day." "Supermarkets are key."

EXHIBIT 4-8
Street Retail

	Prospects	Rating	Ranking
Existing Property Performance	Modestly good	5.50	2nd
New Property Acquisitions	Fair	5.40	3rd
Development	Fair	4.80	5th

Source: *Emerging Trends in Real Estate Europe 2011* survey.

EXHIBIT 4-9
Retail

	Prospects	Rating	Ranking
Existing Property Performance	Fair	5.42	3rd
New Property Acquisitions	Fair	5.45	2nd
Development	Fair	4.55	7th

Source: *Emerging Trends in Real Estate Europe 2011* survey.

EXHIBIT 4-10
Shopping Centres

	Prospects	Rating	Ranking
Existing Property Performance	Fair	5.41	4th
New Property Acquisitions	Fair	5.38	4th
Development	Fair	4.67	6th

Source: *Emerging Trends in Real Estate Europe 2011* survey.

EXHIBIT 4-11
Retail Parks

	Prospects	Rating	Ranking
Existing Property Performance	Fair	5.05	8th
New Property Acquisitions	Fair	5.03	12th
Development	Modestly poor	4.46	10th

Source: *Emerging Trends in Real Estate Europe 2011* survey.

EXHIBIT 4-12
High Street Retail Prime Property Yields

City	Q3 2010 (Percentage)	Q3 2009 (Percentage)	Year-over-Year (Basis Points)
London West End	3.75	4.25	-50
Amsterdam	4.15	4.65	-50
Hamburg	4.50	4.50	0
Munich	4.50	4.50	0
Vienna	4.55	4.70	-15
Zurich	4.60	4.70	-10
Dusseldorf	4.60	4.60	0
Frankfurt	4.60	4.60	0
Paris	4.75	5.50	-75
Brussels	4.75	5.25	-50
Glasgow	4.85	6.50	-165
Berlin	4.90	4.90	0
Stockholm	5.00	5.80	-80
Copenhagen	5.00	5.00	0
Geneva	5.00	5.00	0
Edinburgh	5.25	6.75	-150
Birmingham	5.25	6.25	-100
Manchester	5.25	6.25	-100
Lille	5.25	5.75	-50
Lyon	5.25	5.75	-50
Helsinki	5.50	5.80	-30
Milan	5.50	5.50	0
London City	5.75	6.00	-25
Madrid	5.75	6.00	-25
Rome	5.75	5.90	-15
Oslo	6.00	6.75	-75
Dublin	6.25	6.50	-25
Athens	6.50	5.75	75
Warsaw	6.50	7.00	-50
Prague	6.75	6.75	0
Budapest	7.25	7.75	-50
Lisbon	7.50	7.50	0
Bucharest	11.00	12.00	-100
Moscow	12.00	12.00	0

Source: CB Richard Ellis.

Shopping Centres

Despite the question marks regarding consumer spending, in the end it is the quality of individual asset that counts. "When you buy retail, yes, you buy consumer spending, but you also buy a specific asset in a specific location." "From an investment point of view, it has to be prime, prime, and prime again. Investors need to look at the tenants, leases, management, the long-term sustainability of the mix." "We are big fans of shopping centres, but only if they are right sized and dominant." "Super regional malls will be fine." The outlook for shopping centres is "very good in high-end large shopping malls with premium brands and strong leisure functions."

Given the appeal shopping centres hold for investors, average cap rates dropped by around 60 basis points to 6.7 percent over the past 12 months. Some investors think this product type has become too expensive. "What we see now is an enthusiasm for shopping centres, particularly for the very, very large ones. I am not so sure if they are still adequately priced." "When large specialist operators of shopping centres sell their assets to institutions, I wonder if that has to do with the prices being paid. We are not looking at shopping centres at all."

Retail Warehousing/Parks

This remains the weakest subsector in the retail universe, yet it is not entirely without fans. "We invest in big-box retail, and this has developed in a reasonably good manner. We believe it makes sense." "The big box must be attractive to shop in—[have] good infrastructure." In the main markets—the U.K. and Germany—"the business with big-box retail has picked up significantly." "We are very focused on big-box retail in Germany. They are easy to manage; you get nice yields of 7.5 percent with long leases. [...] You can get debt finance, have a cash flow and no worries for 15 years. That makes a lot of sense." But the usual caveat applies: it is "a sector that is a little overpriced."

A major theme running across all property types is apprehension about secondary and tertiary assets. In the end, it again boils down to stock picking. "I think you have to be very careful with shopping centres. Some will work well, and some will not. The masses of shopping centres will have difficulties." One interviewee predicts "increasing vacancy in the nonprime areas." "Very worried about secondary high street."

Development

Prospects for new developments are limited, with street retail and shopping centres showing better marks than retail parks. Overall, there is potential for repositioning of existing assets. "Opportunities will be within established city areas, repositioning and regenerating land and existing building stock. There [are] still plenty of arbitrage

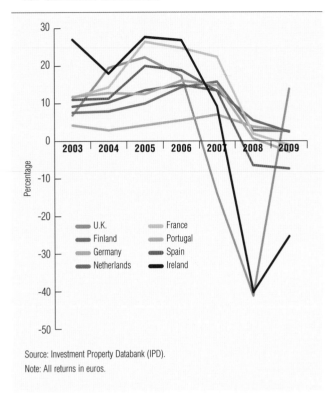

EXHIBIT 4-13
IPD Retail Property Total Returns for Selected Countries

Source: Investment Property Databank (IPD).

Note: All returns in euros.

opportunities on underutilized land in good locations." One interviewee suggests: "Focus on established location instead of new locations." This is echoed by the other comments: "large potential for upgrades of run-down assets"; and "potential in the refurbishment of run-down shopping centres; yet, such investments are very capital intense and require very specific know-how."

With western European markets being increasingly saturated, "you have to go perhaps [to] eastern Europe, southeastern Europe, and Turkey. [But] anything beyond Poland, Hungary, and Czech Republic isn't touched with a barge pole at the moment."

Best Bets

"Germany is currently the most attractive retail market in Europe." "I do see opportunities in retail in Germany." The sentiment is driven by reasonably good economic growth prospects. "The rationale is this: if you have lived in want for two years, there is a certain amount of pent-up demand. It must be met at some point." With Munich, Hamburg, Berlin, and Frankfurt, Germany accounts for four of the top five cities in the survey ranked according to best acquisition prospects for retail. Together they account for more than a quarter of

the retail votes. Despite these positive perceptions, voices of caution are never far off. "On a macro level, it is very difficult to get excited about anyplace, and even in Germany I am not sure stronger growth is creating an environment of high consumer spending. Some retailers are doing well, but [these] tend to be discounters." "The Germans have always preferred to save rather than spend, and I don't see any reason why this should suddenly change."

Proceed with Caution

In the U.K., retail "shopping malls are attractive if they are in South East and are relatively dominant." "London is a country in itself and seems to defy gravity. Regionally, it is going to be ugly. The high street will be really, really pressured to maintain itself." "Consumer demand in the U.K. is an issue, [though] lower employment does not necessarily lead to lower spending at the mall."

Stockholm may experience consolidation because there is "a lot of newly developed retail. Time will tell who owns the right assets that will perform and who owns the bad retail assets. The segment will mature in the years to come."

Avoid

"If you look at southern Europe, they are also more in saving rather than spending mode." In Italy, some shopping centres "suffer from a very quick obsolescence, and at the end of the day, there is a lot of product in this sector." "The big shopping-centres sector is so developed now that there is cannibalization risk." "Retail will be slow in take-up and in investment. It was overdeveloped in the last decade. Some shopping centres [in Portugal will be in] a difficult situation."

Office

City offices are the preferred subsector to invest in. "I see the biggest potential in the office market." "We are absolutely big fans of investing in office." While last year cash flow was king, this year "the focus is mainly on prime locations." "Location has become more important than letting situation; [this] was different before." "Unlike before, you have to pay attention to the quality of the location."

Not only location, but also quality of the building is gaining importance. "Generally, the spread between A-quality properties and the rest will increase." "Flexibility of office space [is] becoming more important as working habits are likely to change going forward." Potential obsolescence is another worry. "There are some assets which in our view will not come back. The peripheral locations of the major cities, spillover locations. [...] Nobody needs these offices anymore." "Demand for office space in mature markets (e.g., western Europe) will likely diminish over the long term due to technological developments, which will enable peo-

EXHIBIT 4-14
Central City Office

	Prospects	Rating	Ranking
Existing Property Performance	Modestly good	5.74	1st
New Property Acquisitions	Modestly good	5.74	1st
Development	Fair	4.96	1st

Source: *Emerging Trends in Real Estate Europe 2011* survey.

EXHIBIT 4-15
Office

	Prospects	Rating	Ranking
Existing Property Performance	Fair	5.33	5th
New Property Acquisitions	Fair	5.12	9th
Development	Modestly poor	4.33	11th (tie)

Source: *Emerging Trends in Real Estate Europe 2011* survey.

EXHIBIT 4-16
Suburban/Out-of-Town Office

	Prospects	Rating	Ranking
Existing Property Performance	Modestly poor	3.86	14th
New Property Acquisitions	Modestly poor	4.19	14th
Development	Poor	3.05	14th

Source: *Emerging Trends in Real Estate Europe 2011* survey.

EXHIBIT 4-17
Office Vacancy/Availability Rates

City	Q3 2010	Q3 2009
Vienna	5.1%	3.7%
Paris CBD	5.3%	4.1%
London (CL)	5.9%	7.2%
Milan	6.1%	6.3%
Ile-de-France	6.8%	6.5%
Munich	7.9%	7.8%
Warsaw	8.0%	7.1%
Hamburg	9.4%	8.2%
Berlin	10.0%	9.8%
Copenhagen	10.1%	7.4%
Madrid	11.3%	10.5%
Brussels	11.8%	10.8%
Prague	13.2%	10.6%
Barcelona	14.3%	9.6%
Moscow	16.1%	17.3%
Frankfurt	17.9%	12.8%
Amsterdam	18.0%	16.3%
Budapest	21.7%	19.4%
Dublin	22.9%	21.6%

Source: CB Richard Ellis.

ple to become more professionally mobile and less dependent on a specific office location." The "shrinking workforce coupled with the `new working´—i.e., working from home—will further impact the office market."

Investor demand is strongly concentrated on capital cities and main cities. Our "focus is on the larger liquid markets. The appetite is for potentially greater risk, but only in really strong locations." Although the clouds of vacancy are still hanging over many rental markets, these do show a silver lining. "We are still sheltered by the fact there is no new supply. There are very few cranes anywhere in Europe; the supply part of the equation is still under control." There is consensus that rents have bottomed out, but opinions on rent increases differ. "The rents have stopped declining in most of the major countries—Germany, France, U.K. I don't see them declining next year [2011]." "No rental growth in the office market, but more occupier demand, more talks. There are people looking for space, signing of leases in Germany, also France; not yet as strong in the U.K." In Germany, "I would not expect substantial rent rises in 2011, but a certain recovery is noticeable." "Rental decline has stopped in almost all markets. In many markets, we see already rising rents—of course, in London and Paris."

Development
Creating a core product in a good—i.e., inner-city—location captures the imagination of developers. "Going forward, redevelopment will be carried out on a larger scale. Prime-location buildings from the '60s to the '80s will be torn down, as they currently do not meet the expectations of the tenants." Another interviewee expects "less new developments, more redevelopments." "Developments in the outskirts are history." "We feel in Germany there is an opportunity to create new product that is environmentally up to scratch because tenants and investors are looking at that these days." This opinion was shared by another survey participant: "Germany is a market where we are more inclined towards development because the end-user demand for Class B space is almost nonexistent, so one has to create the Class A product if you want a guarantee finding tenants."

Curtailing risk is imperative for developers. "For developers, [. . .] the trend will be to reduce risk taking," and they have a strong desire "to proceed to developments only when tenants have been secured in advance." "Development will be less speculative. Banks will be more stringent." "We would not start on a purely speculative building."

Best Bets

"Paris should remain attractive for international investors, especially the prime assets." "France has two completely different markets. We would be more nervous about investing in secondary cities and [are] fully focussed on Paris." "Paris has good long-term prospects. [. . .] We are generally positive on the outlook for rents and decrease of vacancy rates." This view is shared by the more than 10 percent of the survey participants, who voted Paris the top spot for offices. "In Paris, trophy buildings trade at 5 percent or even less. [. . .] There is an expectation for rental growth over the next two to three years."

In Germany, "office is the sector which we believe will do well over the next two to three years." "Occupier markets in Germany are slowly coming back. It's not the case that we are happy every day because tenants are lining up, but [. . .] there is a significant revival of occupier demand." "The absolute winner after the crisis is Germany. The German market has shown stability; the transaction volume is accelerating significantly."

As far as *Emerging Trends Europe* survey participants are concerned, London still holds interesting investment propositions. But it also has become a very expensive place. Among interviewee comments: "London is the top location in Europe";

"London will be good"; "Our opportunity of buying in strong locations cheaply is probably gone, but I am glad we did what we did when we did it"; "In London, more stock is coming to the market, which means that the prices are no longer right. Now, first-class stock is increasingly available. That is a clear signal that prices have reached a level where you have to start being careful"; "In the longer term, we see London at the upper end of what is possible, particularly because we are concerned about the occupier market. Hence, London offices are more of a sell"; and "We invested €400 million in London and have almost sold it all."

Proceed with Caution

Poland drew a lot of attention from interviewees. Among the comments: "We are very bullish for Warsaw and Poland"; "Poland never went into a recession, which makes it unique. It was marked down by the market's perception

EXHIBIT 4-18
IPD Office Property Total Returns for Selected Countries

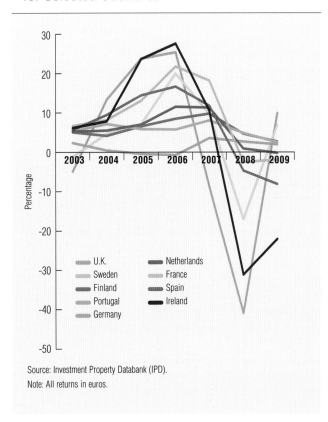

Source: Investment Property Databank (IPD).
Note: All returns in euros.

EXHIBIT 4-19
Office Prime Property Yields

City	Q3 2010 (Percentage)	Q3 2009 (Percentage)	Year-over-Year (Basis Points)
London (West End)	4.00	5.25	-125
Zurich	4.60	4.75	-15
Paris	4.85	5.75	-90
Munich	4.90	5.00	-10
Geneva	5.00	5.25	-25
Hamburg	5.00	5.10	-10
Stockholm	5.00	5.75	-75
Dusseldorf	5.20	5.30	-10
Frankfurt	5.20	5.40	-20
Copenhagen	5.25	5.75	-50
Berlin	5.40	5.50	-10
Amsterdam	5.45	6.15	-70
London (City)	5.50	6.50	-100
Helsinki	5.70	6.00	-30
Milan	5.75	6.00	-25
Rome	5.75	6.00	-25
Barcelona	6.00	6.50	-50
Edinburgh	6.00	6.85	-85
Madrid	6.00	6.50	-50
Oslo	6.00	7.00	-100
Brussels	6.25	6.25	0
Warsaw	6.25	6.75	-50
Athens	6.75	6.25	50
Lisbon	6.75	7.25	-50
Prague	6.85	7.00	-15
Dublin	7.25	7.50	-25
Budapest	7.75	8.00	-25
Moscow	10.50	12.00	-150

Source: CB Richard Ellis.

that it ought to have suffered"; "Poland is interesting for an entry"; "It is the largest economy in the region and has good economic perspectives, but in our view the locations are not quite established"; and "Poland might be possible, but there is enough to do in Germany and France, so you don't have to go to Poland at all costs."

The brave and the courageous have put Spain on their agenda. "In Spain, we are a bit of a cherry picker at the moment. We do believe in the market." Regarding Spain and Italy, "there are problems in these markets, but they are well-established markets with strong domestic players. [We] are buying in Madrid, have bought in Barcelona, and want to do more there, [. . .] but it is, of course, difficult to go into these market with full speed at the moment." "Spain is being looked at very cautiously. I think that the property markets in Madrid and Barcelona will recover very quickly." Others put Spain on the waiting list. "We might be looking to do more investments in Spain once Spain has bottomed out, but definitely not today." "I am surprised about the high prices: doesn't make sense in our view to buy at the current level."

Avoid

"In the Netherlands, the office market is difficult." The fundamentals "in the occupier market are weak, particularly because of the (high) unemployment rates." Overall, "very gloomy perspectives" because there is "oversupply (and additional projects in pipeline), hidden vacancy (not all rented space is occupied), and decreasing demand, partly due to new ways of working and an aging population."

Markets east of Poland are not worth looking at, interviewees said. "No interest in the Balkans or Russia—not an institutional market." "The times when we went to Russia or Croatia, Romania are gone for us." "You can probably make money in Romania and Bulgaria, but it is not our cup of tea."

Nor is there anything outside of capital cities and main cities on investors' radar. "A ticking time bomb is the secondary side. It is a real problem. No investor interest; lenders are not there and [there are] legacy debt issues." "Today we wouldn't touch office assets in secondary markets we might have touched in 2007."

Residential

Despite the growing interest in the commercial markets, residential has a lot going for it. "It is a very stable segment; it is easily quantifiable; it has an intrinsic value—perhaps even a little protection against inflation. The renaissance will continue for a while longer; it is not a temporary phenomenon." "Residential is the sector that a lot of people feel most comfortable about because no matter what people do, they need to have someplace to sleep." "We periodically think about residential in Europe. Actually, it is a super segment; we are all for it."

The low-interest-rate environment is an important driver of investor demand for the residential sector. "As long as interest rates remain low, I can only see growth, especially in prime residential markets." "If you buy residential in a reasonable location and [that is] relatively new, you get a dividend yield of 4 to 4.5 percent. The spread is so attractive for institutions that residential is worthwhile."

Looking further ahead, "urbanisation is, and will be, a significant trend. The strong demand in these cities exceeds the supply and will push up prices." "Urbanisation will continue [and] increase." Market observers lament a "lack of availability of good-quality residential stock." "Assets are hard to find." "A lot of investors are not selling their assets, even if these assets are underperforming. They stick to their investments because they are unable to find alternatives to deploy the equity that would be released." The scarce supply causes prices to rise. "We like residential, but it has become too expensive, particularly in the locations we like." Furthermore, institutional investors require a certain size: "If a portfolio of 10,000 to 15,000 units were to be offered in France, we would seriously look at it, but you do need a certain size."

Demand is strong for apartments for sale. In Germany, "we are seeing this already, and due to the still low level of new development and the good economic development and the rising incomes, this will continue in the next few years." In the big cities, the "rising prices will create opportunities for new development—more potential in the owner/occupier market than for capital investment."

In the U.K., residential space for sale outside London and the South East will suffer. "Sharp cuts in public spending and increasing unemployment will have a negative impact on house prices in the regions in 2011."

EXHIBIT 4-20
Apartment Residential (Rental)

	Prospects	Rating	Ranking
Existing Property Performance	Fair	5.27	6th
New Property Acquisitions	Fair	5.35	5th
Development	Fair	4.84	3rd

Source: *Emerging Trends in Real Estate Europe 2011* survey.

EXHIBIT 4-21
Residential (For Sale)

	Prospects	Rating	Ranking
Existing Property Performance	Fair	4.85	12th
New Property Acquisitions	Fair	5.13	8th
Development	Fair	4.85	2nd

Source: *Emerging Trends in Real Estate Europe 2011* survey.

In the Netherlands, the for-sale residential sector is afflicted by uncertainties regarding future deductibility of interest rates. Potential buyers are taking a wait-and-see attitude and will not commit. Overall, the "market is still waiting for directions; no improvement in 2011."

The availability of mortgages is somewhat patchy. "Banks still like lending on German residential, so you can get decent loans." It gets more difficult in the Netherlands and southern Europe: "The apartment/residential sector will also be slow, basically due to credit squeeze."

Development

Demographic changes makes some developers think about how residential can be further differentiated to meet homeowners' requirements throughout their life span. "We need to be more flexible with what we offer. It [. . .] must cater for the different phases in life—more senior citizens, sheltered housing, and nursing homes; student housing is viewed as an interesting segment; family houses. What is common to all: they will be in inner-city locations."

According to German developers, more than half their inner-city projects are sold to silver-agers—people who move in when they are in their late 50s to early 60s. The question of location and the infrastructure available is a crucial factor for the success of a particular development. People are looking for the infrastructure of inner cities: they are selling their houses in the countryside and in the

suburbs to move downtown. However, selling these family homes can be a tedious exercise because of a lack of potential buyers. "These property are sold, but not at a fantastic price."

Best Bets

In Germany, demand in the main cities will continue to be strong. "Rents will rise, but first and foremost in the main cities, with top rents in the prime locations increasing more than average rents." One interviewee foresees "rental growth in the residential market. This will be followed by capital growth, strong demand for residential in 2011." "Metropolitan regions and rural regions will further drift apart. In the major cities, we will see rent increases and price rises. Berlin/Potsdam will witness the highest increases by far."

While all major German cities attracted high scores as an investment location for apartments, Berlin topped the list as the best location for the sector with 9.8 percent, followed by London with 9.5 percent. "London residential has performed well, with both capital sales and rents rising strongly in 2010." But for 2011 rents, some forecasts show "flat rents and flat capital values for London." "Central London residential is attractive, but no one knows how to access it." "London and South East [are] fine, but other regions poorly performing."

Proceed with Caution

"Stable but always interesting"—so read one of the comments on the residential market in Italy. It is basically a two-tier market with opportunities at either end: "well-off people who require very, very high standards, and controlled-priced apartments—e.g., for students, old people, have-nots." "The residential sector is surprisingly strong in main Italian cities and will remain so." "Demand is focused on good inner-city locations," whereas "peripheral areas are struggling." At the other end of the line, some players are exploring opportunities to create social housing funds.

Avoid

The residential market in Spain is showing no signs of recovery. Major drawbacks include oversupply, the high unemployment rate, the lack of financing, and the elimination of government subsidies for the acquisition of residential space. It "will need a lot of migration to absorb [the oversupply, but] Spain is a growing population and not a declining one, and, hence, the oversupply is a temporary problem."

In Poland, "the residential market has collapsed; no more finance available. [. . .] Some buildings are converted from residential to offices."

EXHIBIT 4-22
IPD Residential Property Total Returns for Selected Countries

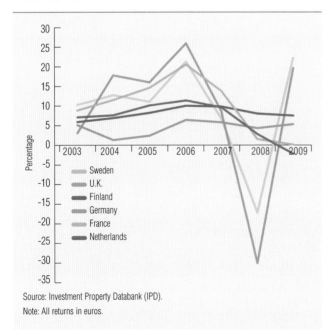

Source: Investment Property Databank (IPD).
Note: All returns in euros.

Hotels

Hardly surprising, there are many investors who are not looking at the hotel sector at all. Among the comments are, "We tend to avoid operating risk associated with real estate assets," and "We are not looking at hotels and other operations-driven investments. We try to avoid investment where others define the outcome."

Those who do like the sector prefer to invest "on the basis of a lease agreement." However, such leases are increasingly difficult to get. "The lack of leasing contracts that are not dependent on results is an obstacle for financing and investment activities as well." "The issue is you have to control the performance-related payment. That is always quite difficult." At the same time, hotel operators wanting to put a growth strategy to work need bank finance. Some new players "facilitate the growth of the brands through franchise and leases for investors."

Still, "hotels can be a good cash flow earner." "If the location is right, business hotels can be complementary investments." One interviewee remarked that her firm is interested in the sector and would "continue focusing on acquiring hotels at discounts to replacement costs in key locations and prime markets with strong macroeconomic and industry fundamentals."

In some markets, trading conditions staged a substantial and a surprisingly quick recovery. Cities like London, Munich, Berlin, and Frankfurt were able to post strong occupancy growth and higher average rates in 2010. Eventually the enhanced performance will help fuel investment activity. "Once you have some months' solid trade performance, [. . .] things are starting to improve. When the recovery comes in operational terms, it comes very, very quickly, [and] investments will come back much more steadily."

The participants in the *Emerging Trends Europe* survey show appetite for the two- to three-star segment. "Germany is undersupplied in the budget sector. Cost of land is such that it makes it still possible to do developments, sold at yields of 6.5 to 7.5 percent." "Standardized products in the two-star and three-star segment squeeze out stand-alone enterprises [in Germany] and are gaining market volume from the upscale segment." In Copenhagen, "new hotel projects will appear in 2011, especially in the two- and three-star segment." One interviewee expects "development of only at most three-star hotels. So far in the key towns [in Poland], the focus was on four- and five-star facilities, and these towns do not offer sufficient reasonably priced solutions." "Outside of London, the prospects are not great, except for budget hotels."

EXHIBIT 4-23
Hotel

	Prospects	Rating	Ranking
Existing Property Performance	Fair	4.96	9th
New Property Acquisitions	Fair	5.18	6th
Development	Modestly poor	4.47	9th

Source: *Emerging Trends in Real Estate Europe 2011* survey.

Best Bets

London and Paris boosted strong trading fundamentals and enjoy continued investor interest. However, hotels "have now gotten to a price point where investors should be thinking, 'I need to start moving to other significant cities.'" Given the somewhat exclusive focus on core markets, it may be difficult to convince investors to venture outside the main cities. "The reason people are paying that money in London and Paris is that perhaps they had their fingers burnt in more exciting economies and they appreciate buying real estate in a major capital city in 2011."

Just barely a year ago, Berlin was plagued by potential oversupply. Now, the city "has done a fantastic job in trying to launch the city as a short stay destination. [. . .] You are starting to really benefit from seven-day-a-week trade." But Munich, Frankfurt, and Hamburg are also showing rising room rates and increased occupancy.

Markets to Watch

"Poland is an oasis in the eastern half of Europe. Cities such as Gdansk [and] Warsaw are doing incredibly well." In 2012, Polish hotels should benefit from the European soccer championship.

Market observers in Moscow are positive about hotels. "The increase in occupancy seen in 2010 will continue into 2011." There is "still [a] lack of three-star product for a few years to come. The demand is huge." The falling land prices in Moscow may help alleviate the shortage and open up opportunities for development, but at present there are "no new developments in Moscow—nothing going on."

Avoid

As for southern Europe, "there is still a bit of a way to go for the likes of Greece, Spain, and Portugal. Life will continue to be difficult for a while, I am afraid." The Spanish market "will be very negative. There is a surplus of offer in the market that needs to be adjusted. [The] largest Spanish hotel chains are closing assets in Spain and going to other countries." Hotels on the coast "depend on the evolution of the German and English economies."

Industrial/Distribution

Logistics "suffered a massive blow." "Logistics has been a difficult sector: rents have fallen, vacancy risen." But things are looking brighter. "Over the last six to 12 months, [. . .] there has been a very positive take-up in the markets overall. We returned to positive net absorption, consistent across Europe." "There is significant improved demand—occupiers taking advantage of the reduced rental costs and increased availability of new product."

How investors weathered the storm depended on the quality of their assets. "If you get the location right in terms of transport connection, then you have actually quite a good investment, which can be re-let in the long run. Rents are not skyrocketing, but also not plummeting." "Apart from a few notable exceptions, we have focused on top-quality properties—brand new buildings and in locations which we knew to be a must—and they came through the crisis relatively unscathed." "The industrial/logistics market has been performing relatively well also during the crisis as it is a cash-flow product. Especially the high-end distribution centres are—and will be—in demand."

"You have got an increased interest from investors looking to pursue and invest in prime product." But some may need to be nudged a little. As a fund manager observes, "We think logistics is very exciting, but find it difficult to convince our clients. They don't like logistics just yet; hence, we are working on this subject."

The profiles of Europe's logistic markets vary widely. In the U.K., industrial and warehouse distribution are fit for institutional investment, while in continental Europe, institutional interest remains patchy. "We always have an eye on logistics and light industrial. It is hard to piece together enough critical mass in Germany. U.K. institutions would take us out of our messy industrial estates, whereas even the most aggressive institutional buyer from Germany has no interest to own that stuff. It is quite a cultural difference that we are conscious of. Even in France it works. The institutions are interested in that sector because of the yields. They'll be buying stuff at 8.5 to 10 percent yields."

"As soon as you have a real core product, it becomes expensive." Cap rates are lowest in the U.K. "at 6 or just below 6 percent; prime in France and Germany is probably 7 to 7.25 percent; and prime in central Europe is probably 8 to 8.25 percent," with potential for some yield compression in central Europe.

Development

In the U.K., there is a wall of money building up and waiting to be invested in the sector. "Because of the limited availability of prime product, some of that capital will look to joint venture with development companies to get access to new developments." Preferred locations are London and

EXHIBIT 4-24
Warehouse Distribution

	Prospects	Rating	Ranking
Existing Property Performance	Fair	5.16	7th
New Property Acquisitions	Fair	5.16	7th
Development	Fair	4.52	8th

Source: *Emerging Trends in Real Estate Europe 2011* survey.

EXHIBIT 4-25
Industrial/Distribution

	Prospects	Rating	Ranking
Existing Property Performance	Fair	4.91	11th
New Property Acquisitions	Fair	5.07	11th
Development	Modestly poor	4.33	11th (tie)

Source: *Emerging Trends in Real Estate Europe 2011* survey.

EXHIBIT 4-26
Manufacturing

	Prospects	Rating	Ranking
Existing Property Performance	Modestly poor	4.25	13th
New Property Acquisitions	Modestly poor	4.36	13th
Development	Modestly poor	3.87	13th

Source: *Emerging Trends in Real Estate Europe 2011* survey.

South East and strong regional hubs—for instance, the Midlands golden triangle.

Opportunities may arise to turn around some of the nonprime assets into core assets over a period of time. "Secondary and tertiary stock is a very, very broad range of product; some of that secondary product will become increasingly attractive. The challenge in accessing secondary product is matching pricing and returns in a world where banks are generally unprepared to lend on anything less than a five-year lease term to a well-located product."

Manufacturing

Given the enormous concentration on core, the comments on the sector were very few and far between. The outlook for the sector is "modestly poor." Fresh impetus may come from the secondary sector wanting to cash in on real estate assets, coupled with increasing institutional demand, notably in Germany. "This will be driven by the need of institutions to find performance, but it is not a story for 2011." "Larger medium-sized companies will go for sale and leaseback. The portfolios are partly characterised by industrial issues, not necessarily offices only."

Best Bets

"There is significant U.K. domestic investment capital queued up, less prepared to look to continental Europe for investment opportunity and still very keen to focus on the U.K."

France remains a very attractive country for both investment and for development. "It has a big population, there are big population concentrations, and there is a large consumer market."

Though the "Nordics aren't a part of the world, in my mind, that is ever going to set the world alight, it is a good, solid, stable environment for investment and development."

EXHIBIT 4-27
Industrial Prime Property Yields

City	Q3 2010 (Percentage)	Q3 2009 (Percentage)	Year-over-Year (Basis Points)
Geneva	6.50	6.75	-25
London Heathrow	6.50	7.00	-50
Oslo	6.75	7.75	-100
Birmingham	6.85	7.75	-90
Dusseldorf	7.00	7.25	-25
Frankfurt	7.00	7.25	-25
Hamburg	7.00	7.25	-25
Manchester	7.00	7.75	-75
Munich	7.00	7.25	-25
Stockholm	7.00	7.75	-75
Zurich	7.00	7.00	0
Paris	7.15	8.25	-110
Berlin	7.25	7.50	-25
Brussels	7.25	7.60	-35
Edinburgh	7.25	7.75	-50
Glasgow	7.25	8.00	-75
Helsinki	7.25	7.25	0
Vienna	7.30	7.60	-30
Copenhagen	7.75	7.75	0
Lisbon	7.75	8.25	-50
Milan	7.75	8.00	-25
Rome	7.75	8.00	-25
Warsaw	7.75	8.75	-100
Amsterdam	7.80	7.90	-10
Madrid	8.00	8.25	-25
Athens	8.50	8.15	35
Bratislava	8.75	8.75	0
Prague	8.75	8.75	0
Dublin	9.00	9.00	0
Budapest	9.25	9.50	-25
Bucharest	10.50	10.50	0
Istanbul	11.00	12.00	-100
Moscow	13.50	14.00	-50

Source: CB Richard Ellis.

Proceed with Caution

"The German economy will remain strong, and there is going to be plenty of opportunity for new development over the course of the next couple of years." Others take a more cautious stance. "You mustn't forget that there is still enough space available and that new developments can be built on greenfield sites at any time. I think in the future one has to think twice: if you can get high-quality office or retail at around 6 percent, do you really want to pick up a warehouse at the same price?"

Currently, the Polish market is marked by oversupply; new development is limited to build-to-suit facilities. "No speculative developments [and] very high vacancy will have downward pressure on rents," but "surprisingly, the investment activity on this market is higher than expected."

"Italy is kind of interesting. Its lack of transparency makes it an unknown quantity in terms of opportunity and risk. It'll just continue to bounce along." Because there is an oversupply of new logistic premises in some locations in Italy now, leasing is quite slow. "Leasing activity continues to be driven by cost-saving and space-rationalization strategies, particularly in Milan." "Logistic firms are coming back. They need good locations and new products—not too expensive, but solid." Hence, there is a space for build-to-suit assets.

EXHIBIT 4-28
IPD Industrial Property Total Returns for Selected Countries

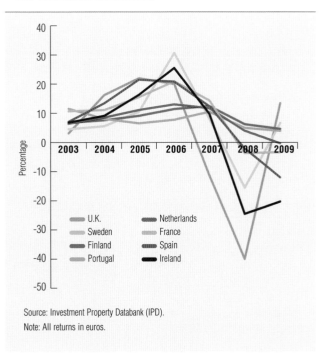

Source: Investment Property Databank (IPD).
Note: All returns in euros.

Avoid

Southern and eastern Europe are not considered investment alternatives. "Spain has its own challenges." In Italy, older stock in peripheral locations hampered by lack of infrastructure "will suffer a lot, even if rent level is lower." "Russia is interesting, particularly Moscow, but its lack of transparency in general makes it challenging. We don't believe there is sufficient risk premium to invest there today."

Mixed Use

Some comments suggest that the mixed use sector is not an investment category in its own right. Negative remarks outweigh positive ones. Among the observations: "Weak prospects. Not an investment asset"; "Mixed risk profile, uncertain exit"; "Not an investment asset, […] hard to predict an exit"; "Not very positive, as this kind of investment mixes two risks and investors just want one risk to deal with"; and "Some investors such as German institutional investors rather prefer `pure play´ investments."

Certain combinations make better bedfellows than others. "Total mixed use makes little sense," one interviewee said. Another observed the potential of various mixes: "Office and retail—OK; hotel and luxury apartments—OK; office and residential—no!"

On a slightly more positive note and probably more of a medium- to long-term trend, urban renewal schemes may be able to create investment opportunities. "Urban quality is determined by property quality, and the real estate industry is a key driver." Some of these brownfield conversions are located just a stone's throw from the inner city. As sustainability concerns feature more strongly in development plans, the regeneration of inner-city property may create new space for working and living. "There will be a new generation of workers in cities, so [developers] need to offer them something attractive, especially where there is a high cost of living." "Mixed use may offer an answer to how growth in quality can be achieved in an economic environment, which is otherwise not marked by growth." "Real estate investment companies have to think in terms of mixed-use city-area developments."

EXHIBIT 4-29
Mixed Use

	Prospects	Rating	Ranking
Existing Property Performance	Fair	4.94	10th
New Property Acquisitions	Fair	5.07	10th
Development	Fair	4.84	4th

Source: *Emerging Trends in Real Estate Europe 2011* survey.

Best Bets

Some urban renewal schemes are underway in Germany—for instance, Europaviertel in Frankfurt and Europacity in Berlin. Apart from offices, they include a substantial amount of residential use and some retail space, and thus facilitate urbanisation.

In London, "prospects for mixed-use schemes are reasonably good." Elsewhere in the U.K., mixed-use projects are less common, "because presales on residential—e.g., to buy-to-let investors buying off plan, and pre-lets to commercial tenants in the commercial [part of the development]—aren't happening. Tenant demand for commercial is too weak outside West End/City London markets."

Markets to Watch

In Portugal, there may be opportunities for redevelopment and urban renewal schemes. "The revitalization of some old urban quarters linked with some social programs could drive some improvement." Again, this is more of a medium-term proposition. There will probably be more interest for "a greater focus on urban rehabilitation and smart growth instead of new developments and urban sprawl."

In major Italian cities, there is room "to develop new schemes and to regenerate mixed use in town."

Avoid

Mixed-use development is not an option for Poland. "Investors do not like this product, and therefore there is a very limited number of such developments." "Funds want to split the ownership of the properties and invest only in a given type. This results in co-ownership issues and difficult management."

Niche Products

As already noted in this chapter, demographic changes have arrived on investors' radar screens. New types of seniors' living facilities might emerge, reflecting the needs of an aging European population and the desire of the elderly to stay in their own homes as long as possible. This ties into developers' observations of older people buying inner-city flats. Still, "it is very difficult to forecast a trend for old-age residential and nursing facilities, whether you are taken care of at home or in a nursing home. It has to do with politics, what is subsidised. Demand is difficult to gauge." For people needing full-time care, "the market for nursing houses is going to evolve." Institutions are likely to focus on the classic nursing home. For an established asset, a yield of 8 percent is considered risk appropriate. It can "be an interesting complementary investment."

Interviewees

Aareal Bank AG
Norbert Herrmann

Aberdeen AM
Bob Reidsma

Aberdeen Asset Management Sweden AB
Magnus Kenning

Aberdeen Property Investors
Alessandro Bronda
Andrew Smith

ABN-AMRO MeesPierson
Pieter Akkerman

Acciona Inmobiliaria
Isabel Antúnez

AEW Europe
Dr. Mahdi Mokrane

AFIAA Investment AG
Hans Brauwers

AIB Polonia Property Funds
Miroslaw Januszko

AIG Lincoln Romania
Sven Lemmes

Akademiska Hus AB
Gunnar Oders

Aleph SGR
Federico Musso

Allianz Real Estate
Olivier Piani

Altera Vastgoed NV
Cyril van den Hoogen

AM
Roel Vollebregt

AMF-Pension
Martin Tufvesson

Annexum Invest BV
Huib Boissevain

Apollo Global Management
Roger Orf

AREA Property Partners
Jon H. Zehner

ASR
Dick Gort

Athens Economics
Dika Agapitidou

Atlas Management
Christian Melgaard

Atrium Ljungberg
Anders Nylander

AtticaBank Properties
Theodoros Glavas

Avestus Capital Partners
Roger Dunlop

Aviva Investors
Ian Womack

AXA Investment Managers Schweiz
Rainer Suter

AXA Real Estate
Kiran Patel

AXA Real Estate Investment Managers
Anne T. Kavanagh
Pierre Vaquier

Banca IMI
Pietro Mazzi
Roberto Ponta

Banif Investment Managers
Luís Saramago Carita

Bank Austria Real Invest–Member of UniCredit Group
Harald Kopertz

Bank of Ireland Real Estate Management
Peter Collins

Bank Zachodni WBK SA
Marcin Dubno

Barrington Holdings Sp. z o.o.
Adam Grabski

Bayerische Landesbank
Ingo Glaeser

Beacon Capital Partners France
Jean-Marc Besson

Beni Stabili
Alexandre Astier

Benson Elliot
Marc Mogull

Blackstone Real Estate
Chad R. Pike

BNP Paribas Real Estate
Michele Cibrario

Bouwfonds Real Estate Investment Management
Jean Klijnen

Bouwinvest
Dick van Hal
Karen Huizer

Brookfield Europe
Shane Kelly

BulwienGesa AG
Andreas Schulten

BZ WBK AIB Towarzystwo Funduszy Inwestycyjnych
Agnieszka Jachowicz

CA Immobilien AG
Mag. Wolfhard Fromwald

Capital Marketing Group
Christophe G. de Taurines

The Carlyle Group
Robert Hodges
Dr. Wulf Meinel
Eric Sasson

Castellum AB
Henrik Saxborn

Catalyst Capital
Fabrice de Clermont-Tonnerre

Catella Real Estate AG KAG
Axel Wünnenberg

CBRE
Francesco Abba
Georg Fichtinger
Pedro Seabra
Mike Strong

CBRE–Axies
Nicholas Chatzitsolis

CBRE Investors–MRM
Jacques Blanchard
Nick Preston

Cegereal
Raphaël Tréguier

Close Brothers Group
Nigel Ashfield
Chris Taylor

CMS Cameron McKenna
Vladislav Sourkov

Colony Capital
Serge Platonow

Cordea Savills
Piergiulio Dentice di Accadia
Justin O'Connor
Cristiano Ronchi

Corio
Gerard Groener

Cornerstone Real Estate Advisors Europe
Iain Reid

CORPUS SIREO Asset Management
Ingo Hartlief

CR Capital Real Estate AG
Thomas Ehrich

Credit Suisse
Ian Marcus
Rainer Scherwey

**Crimson Investment
    Management–Carlyle Group**
Carlos Moedas

Cushman & Wakefield
Jef Van Doorslaer
Timothy Millard
Joachim Sandberg

Dan-Ejendomme A/S
Henrik Dahl Jeppesen

De Alliantie
Arnold Pureveen

Deka Bank
Dr. Matthias Danne
Mark Titcomb

DELA Vastgoed
Pieter Loeffen

**Deutsche Hypothekenbank
    (Actien-Gesellschaft)**
Dr. Jürgen Allerkamp

Development Solutions
AlexeyBlanin

DKB Immobilien AG
Wolfgang Schnurr

DLJ Real Estate Capital Partners
Carla Giannini

Dolphin Capital Partners
Michael Tsirikos

Drago Capital
José García Cedrún

DTZ
Jean-Pierre Lequeux

DTZ Asset Management
Patrice Genre

EHL Immobilien
Michael Ehlmaier
Franz Pöltl

Ellwanger & Geiger, Private Bank
Helmut Kurz

Eurohypo
Patrick Lesur
Max Sinclair

Eurohypo–Portuguese Branch
Carlos Leiria-Pinto

Europa Capital Partners
Nic Fox
Charles Graham

Extensa Group
Daniel Geerts

**F&C Portugal, Gestão de
    Patrimónios**
António Pena do Amaral

Fabrica Immobiliare
Marco Doglio

FastPartner
Daniel Gerlach
Sven-Olof Johansson

Ferrovial
Alvaro Echániz

FGH Bank
Roel van de Bilt

FIMIT SGR
Andrea Cornetti

Finstroy Holding
Sergey Khramov

First Atlantic Real Estate
Cristina Bianchi

Foncière INEA
Philippe Rosio

Foncière Paris France
Didier Brethes
Jean-Paul Dumortier

Franklin Templeton Institutional
Raymond Jacobs

FundBox, SGFII
Rui Alpalhão

Gabetti Property Solutions Agency
Giorgio Lazzaro

**Générale Continentale
    Investissements**
Paul Raingold
Raphaël Raingold

Generali Deutschland
Barbara Deisenrieder

Generali Immobiliare Italia
Giovanni Maria Paviera

GE Real Estate
Karol Pilniewicz
Lennart Sten
Rainer Thaler

GMP
Francisco Montoro
Diego Valiente

Goldman Sachs International
Edward Siskind

Goodman
Danny Peeters

Grainger Trust
Andrew Pratt

Great Portland Estates
Timon Drakesmith

GreenOak Real Estate Advisors
John Carrafiell

Groupama
François Netter

Grupo Lar
Luis J. Pereda

**Hamburg Trust Grundvermögen und
    Anlage GmbH**
Dr. Joachim Seeler

Hardstone
Spiros Seretis

Henderson Global Investors
Patrick Sumner

**Hermes Real Estate Investment
    Management**
Tatiana Bosteels

**HIH Hamburgische Immobilien
    Handlung GmbH**
Erik Marienfeldt

Hines
Lee Timmins

Hines Europe
Lars Huber

Hines Italia
Manfredi Catella

Hochtief Projektentwicklung GmbH
Lars N. Follmann

HSH Nordbank
Peter Lilja

**HVS Consulting and Valuation–
    London**
Tim Smith

Hypo Real Invest
Herwig Teufelsdorfer

The IBUS Company
Pepijn Morshuis

Icade
Nicolas Dutreuil

Il Forte SpA
Alberto Lupi

Immoeast
Manfred Witschnigg

ING Bank Hipoteczny
Michal Rokosz
Wlodzimierz Skonieczny

ING Real Estate Development
Hein Brand

ING Real Estate Finance
Rudolf Molkenboer

ING Real Estate Investment Management
Hans Copier

Inmobiliaria Colonial
Pere Viñolas

Inmobiliaria del Sur
Ricardo Pumar

Internos Real Investors
Jos Short

Invesco Real Estate
William Ertz
Doris Pittlinger
Alexander Taft

Investire Immobiliare
Domenico Bilotta
Dario Valentino

IPD
Alasdair Evans
Peter Hobbs

IVG Immobilien AG
Thomas Beyerle
Frédéric Heitz
Guido Pinol

IVG Institutional Funds
Bernhard Berg

IVG Real Estate Belgium SA
Bernhard Veithen

JER Partners
Chester Barnes

Jeudan
Per W. Hallgren

Jones Lang LaSalle
Olivier Bastin
Charles Boudet
Patrick Parkinson
Tomasz Puch

JP Morgan Real Assets
Peter Reilly

Kadans Vastgoed
Michel Leemhuis

KBC Real Estate
Hubert De Peuter

King Sturge
Jaroslaw Wnuk

Klépierre
Frédéric De Klopstein

KLP Eiendom
Gorm Gudim

Knight Frank
Dorota Latkowska-Diniejko

Korn Ferry
Bill Kistler

Kungsleden
Thomas Erséus

KVWS
Alfred Vos

La Caixa
David Rico

Lamda Development
Alexandros Kokkidis

Landesbank Baden-Württemberg–LBBW
Pascale Ben Sadou

Landesbank Hessen-Thüringen Girozentrale
Johann Berger

LaSalle Investment Management
Amy Aznar
David Ironside
Simon Marrison
Claus Thomas

Laurentius
Joop Peijen

Lazard & Co
Giacomo Liberti

Leasinvest Real Estate
Jean Louis Appelmans

Legal & General
Bill Hughes

Leyten
Rob de Jong

LHI Leasing
Robert Soethe

L.P. Ellinas Group
Loucas Ellinas

LSI
Ernst Kramer

MAB Development Group
Jan G.F. Eijkemans

MEAG Munich ERGO AssetManagement GmbH
Stefan Krausch

MGPA
Laurent Luccioni

Mn Services
Herman Gelauff
Richard van Ovost

Moorfields
Graham Stanley

Morgan Stanley
Olivier de Poulpiquet
Struan Robertson
Donato Saponara

Multi Vastgoed
Eric van Duren

NAI Estate Fellows
Rafał Mateusiak

Natixis Capital Partners
Stephan Fritsch

New Century Holdings / Agroterra
Pavel Remezov

Niam
Fredrik Jonsson

NIBC
Jan-Jaap Meindersma

Norfin
Bernardo Pinto Basto

NS Poort
Jaap Reijnders

OMERS
Simon Marriott

Orion Capital Managers
Bruce Bossom
Aref Lahham
Van Stults

Ote Estate (member of OTE Group)
Krysta Petropoulou
Christini Spanoudaki

Pacific Investments
Gerald Parkes

Palatium Investment Management
Neil Lawson-May
Paul Rivlin

Panattoni
Robert Dobrzycki

Pangaea REIC
Aristotelis Karytinos

Park Hill Real Estate Group
Audrey Klein

PATRIZIA Acquisition & Consulting GmbH
Klaus Kümmerle

PGGM
Guido Verhoef

Ping Properties
Robert Kohsiek

Pinnacle Real Estate Innovation
Martin Carr

**Pohjola Property
 Management Limited**
Markku Mäkiaho

PointPark Properties
Ian Worboys

Polis Fondi SGR
Paolo Berlanda
Gustavo Tani

Polish Properties Sp. z o.o.
Chris Grzesik

Pradera
Colin Campbell

Pramerica Real Estate Investors
Eric Adler
Thomas Hoeller
Rüdiger Schwarz

Prelios SGR
Paola Del Monte
Rodolfo Misitano

ProLogis Europe
Philip Dunne

ProLogis Poland Management
Bartosz Mierzwiak

Property Partners
Marc Baertz
Vincent Bechet

**Prudential Property Investment
 Managers**
Anne Koeman
Paul McNamara

PZU Asset Management
Włodzimierz Kocoń

Quares
Ralph Willems

Quintain Estates and Development
Rebecca Worthington

**Raiffeisen Immobilien
 Kapitalanlage-Gesellschaft**
Hubert Voegel

Raven Russia Property Management
Adrian Baker

REALIA Business, S.A.
Jaime Lloréns

Redevco Central Europe
Jörg F. Bitzer

Retail Estates
Jan de Nijs

Riksbyggen
Sten-Åke Karlsson

Risanamento SpA
Davide Albertini Petroni

Rockspring
Arnaud le Mintier

**Rockspring Property
 Investment Manager**
Stuart Reid

Royal Bank Scotland
Mike McNamara

RREEF
Dr. Georg Allendorf
Ismael Clemente
Gianluca Muzzi

Saxo Properties A/S
Claus Klostermann

Scenari Immobiliari
Mario Breglia

Schiphol Real Estate
Maarten Brink
André van den Berg

**Schroder Property
 Kapitalanlagegesellschaft mbH**
Michael Ruhl

SEB Asset Management
Barbara Knoflach

Secure Management
Lambros Anagnostopoulos
Constantin Pechlivanidis

Sehested Consulting
Michael Sehested

Serenissima SGR
Luca Giacomelli

Sierra Management Greece
Pavlina Chandras

Signa Recap Germany
Lars Herrstroem

**Skanska Commercial
 Development Europe**
Richard Hultin

SNS Property Finance
Guido Buurlage

SRV Russia
Timo Hokkanen

Starwood Capital
Sean Arnold

Sveafastigheter
Johanna Skogestig

Testa Inmobiliaria
Daniel Loureda

Tishman Speyer
Michael Spies

TLG Immobilien
Niclas Karoff

The Townsend Group
Adam Calman

Trastor REIC
Kenny Evangelou

Tristan Capital Partners
Ric Lewis

UBS Real Estate France
Adrien Blanc

Unibail Rodamco
Peter van Rossum

UniCredit Bank Austria AG
Reinhard Madlencnik

Valad France
Gilles Vaissié

Valad Property Group
Martyn McCarthy
Mark McLaughlin

Vasakronan
Anders Ahlberg

VastNed Retail NV
Arnaud du Pont

Vesteda
Luurt van der Ploeg

Vorm Holding
Daan van der Vorm

**Warburg-Henderson
 Kaitalanlagegesellschaft für
 Immobilien mbH**
Henning Klöppelt

Warner Estate Holdings Plc
Robert Game

WDP (Warehouses De Pauw)
Joost Uwents

Westdeutsche ImmobilienBank AG
Maciej Tuszynski

West Immo
Peter Denton

Westimmo (West LB) Spain
Lee Mays

WonenBreburg
Ton Streppel

Woonbron
Johan Over de Vest

Ymere
P.P. Ebbelinghaus

Züblin Immobilien Holding AG
Bruno Schefer

Zurich Insurance Company
Barbara V. Stuber

Sponsoring Organizations

PwC's real estate practice assists real estate investment advisers, real estate investment trusts, public and private real estate investors, corporations, and real estate management funds in developing real estate strategies; evaluating acquisitions and dispositions; and appraising and valuing real estate. Its global network of dedicated real estate professionals enables it to assemble for its clients the most qualified and appropriate team of specialists in the areas of capital markets, systems analysis and implementation, research, accounting, and tax.

Global Real Estate Leadership Team

Kees Hage
Global Real Estate Leader
PwC (Luxembourg)

Uwe Stoschek
Global Real Estate Tax Leader
European, Middle East, and Africa Real Estate Leader
PwC (Germany)

K.K. So
Asia Pacific Real Estate Tax Leader
PwC (China)

Timothy Conlon
United States Real Estate Leader
PwC (U.S.)

Barry Benjamin
Global Asset Management Leader
PwC (U.S.)

John Parkhouse
European, Middle East, and Africa Asset Management Leader
PwC (Luxembourg)

www.pwc.com

The mission of the Urban Land Institute is to provide leadership in the responsible use of land and in creating and sustaining thriving communities worldwide. ULI is committed to

■ Bringing together leaders from across the fields of real estate and land use policy to exchange best practices and serve community needs;

■ Fostering collaboration within and beyond ULI's membership through mentoring, dialogue, and problem solving;

■ Exploring issues of urbanization, conservation, regeneration, land use, capital formation, and sustainable development;

■ Advancing land use policies and design practices that respect the uniqueness of both built and natural environments;

■ Sharing knowledge through education, applied research, publishing, and electronic media; and

■ Sustaining a diverse global network of local practice and advisory efforts that address current and future challenges.

Established in 1936, the Institute today has nearly 30,000 members worldwide, representing the entire spectrum of the land use and development disciplines. ULI relies heavily on the experience of its members. It is through member involvement and information resources that ULI has been able to set standards of excellence in development practice. The Institute has long been recognized as one of the world's most respected and widely quoted sources of objective information on urban planning, growth, and development.

Patrick L. Phillips
Chief Executive Officer, Urban Land Institute

ULI Center for Capital Markets and Real Estate
Dean Schwanke
Senior Vice President and Executive Director

Urban Land Institute
1025 Thomas Jefferson Street, NW
Suite 500 West
Washington, DC 20007
202-624-7000
www.uli.org

ULI Europe
London
44 (0) 20 7487 9570
www.uli.org/europe